Music Express

Year 4

LESSON PLANS, RECORDINGS, ACTIVITIES, PHOTOCOPIABLES AND VIDEOCLIPS

Compiled by Maureen Hanke Illustrated by Alison Dexter Edited by Emily Haward

A & C Black • London

Contents

First published 2002
Reprinted 2003
by A & C Black Publishers Ltd
37, Soho Square, London W1D 3QZ

ISBN 0 7136 6232 8

Teaching text © Maureen Hanke 2002
Unit headings, unit summary text, learning objectives and outcomes © Qualifications and Curriculum Authority, 2000
CD/Videoclips compilation © A & C Black 2002
Edited by Emily Haward
Designed by Jocelyn Lucas
Cover illustration © Alex Ayliffe 2002
Inside illustrations © Alison Dexter 2002
Audio CD sound engineering by Stephen Chadwick
Videoclips filmed and edited by Jamie Acton-Bond
CD-ROM post production by Ian Shepherd
at Sound Recording Technology

Printed in Great Britain by Caligraving Ltd, Thetford, Norfolk

A & C Black uses paper produced with elemental chlorine-free pulp, harvested from managed sustainable forests.

A CIP catalogue record for this book is available from the British Library.

Introduction

About Music Express

Music Express provides teaching activities that are imaginative, inspiring and fun.

It has been written especially for classroom teachers. It is:

- user-friendly;
- well planned;
- fully resourced, and
- no music reading is required.

Using Music Express as a scheme of work

National Curriculum

Music Express fulfils the requirements of the Music National Curriculum of England, of Wales and of Northern Ireland and the 5-14 National Guidelines for Scotland.

Learning with ***Music Express***, children will gain a broad and balanced musical education. They will:

- learn about and sing songs from around the world including the British Isles;
- learn about music from different periods and genres;
- enjoy music lessons with a balance of listening, composing, performing and appraising.

A steady progression plan has been built into ***Music Express***, both within each book and from one year to the next, ensuring consistent musical development.

Opportunities are identified throughout for evaluating the children's work and monitoring their progress.

The English QCA scheme of work for music

Music Express is based on the structure of the QCA scheme of work. It uses the same unit headings, and provides activities for all the learning objectives and outcomes.

The teaching activities in ***Music Express*** have been drawn from and inspired by A & C Black's extensive classroom music resources.

The units

There are six units in each book. Below is a list of the units in ***Music Express Year 4***, as described by the QCA:

Play it again (Unit 10)
'This unit develops children's ability to create simple rhythmic patterns and perform them rhythmically using notation as a support.'

The class orchestra (Unit 11)
'This unit develops children's ability to create, combine and perform rhythmic and melodic material as part of a class performance of a song.'

Dragon scales (Unit 12)
'This unit develops children's ability to recognise, and use scales, and create short melodies and accompaniments.'

Painting with sound (Unit 13)
'This unit develops children's ability to create, perform and analyse expressive compositions and extend their sound vocabulary.'

Salt pepper vinegar mustard (Unit 14)
'This unit develops children's ability to recognise and explore some characteristics of [signals]. It consolidates their sense of pulse and ability to perform with others.'

Animal magic (Unit 9)
'This unit develops children's ability to create, perform and analyse short descriptive compositions that combine sounds, movements and words.'

The lessons

Each unit is divided into six, weekly lessons, which are intended to be taught over a half term.

There are three activities per lesson which may be taught in one longer music lesson, or over three shorter lessons to suit your timetable.

Planning

The CD-ROM

The CD-ROM provides a medium term plan and six, weekly lesson plans for each unit. These may be printed out to go in your planning folder.

Whilst it is not necessary when teaching the activities to have the lesson plan alongside, it contains useful information for preparing your lesson. This includes:

- the learning objectives and outcomes;
- a list of the resources and minimal preparation you will need to do before the lesson;
- a vocabulary section which defines the musical terms appropriate to the lesson;
- a suggestion of ways to provide differentiated support for particular activities;
- a lesson extension - a suggestion for taking the lesson further with individuals or the whole class. (The extension activities are particularly useful when teaching a mixed year-group class as they extend the older and/or more able children.)

The book

The book provides step by step teaching notes for each lesson. These are written to be as easy to follow as possible.

There are photocopiables to supplement many of the activities.

Preparation

Music Express is designed to minimise your preparation time.

Look out for the icons next to the activity headings which indicate things you need to prepare.

Key to icons

Photocopiable icon: some activities require photocopies or activity cards to be made from a particular photocopiable.

CD icon: you will need to have access to a CD player for an activity.

Videoclip and picture icons: you will need to have access to a computer for an activity to show videoclips and pictures on the CD-ROM. (You might like to use a computer-compatible projector to show the videoclips and pictures on a screen for the whole class to see more easily.)

Other resources

Classroom percussion

You will need to have a range of classroom percussion instruments available.

Many activities suggest several members of the class playing instruments at the same time. If necessary, pupils could share instruments and take turns to play.

Specific activities recommend the instruments you will need, but you should use the instruments that you have available.

For a class of 30 pupils, aim to have at least the following:

- Tuned percussion
  - 1 alto xylophone
  - 1 alto metallophone
  - 1 set of chime bars
  - a selection of beaters
- A range of untuned percussion instruments, eg
  - tambours
  - drums
  - wood blocks
  - cabassas
  - maracas

- Other interesting soundmakers, eg
  - ocean drum
  - rainmaker
  - whistles
  - wind chimes
- Electronic keyboards are a very useful resource and should be included whenever possible.

Instrumental lessons

Whenever appropriate, invite members of the class who are having instrumental lessons to bring their instruments into classroom music lessons.

If you are not sure which notes particular instruments use, ask the child's instrumental teacher.

Recording and evaluating

Recording on cassette or video

Have a cassette recorder and blank audio cassettes available during your music lessons. Recording pupils' work is important for monitoring their progress.

Children enjoy listening to their performances and contributing to the evaluation of their own and their classmates' work.

Many activities include movement as well as music. If you have a video camera available, video the performance. If not, invite members of your class or another class to watch and offer feedback.

Help for teachers

Teaching tips and background information

These are provided throughout next to the activity or activities to which they refer.

Dance and movement

Encourage movement in activities even when it is not mentioned - it is an important means of musical learning.

Group work

The activities suggest appropriate group sizes. Be flexible, especially if your class has little or no experience of group work. Group work may be introduced into classroom music lessons gradually. Those activities which suggest group work may also be managed as whole class activities.

Teaching songs

We hope that teachers will lead the singing with their own voices, particularly with younger children. But in all instances we have assumed that the teacher will use the CD.

If you feel confident, teach yourself a song using the CD and then teach it to the children.

To rehearse songs with your class without the CD, you might:

- sing the melody without the words, to lah or dee;
- chant the rhythm of the words;
- sing the song line by line for the children to copy.

Teachers' videoclips

There are seventeen videoclips on the CD-ROM that demonstrate useful teaching techniques to use in class music lessons.

Clip	Contents
T 01	The Music Express Song
T 02	Teaching a song line by line
T 03	Demonstrating pitch with hand
T 04	Starting together: speed and starting note
T 05	Internalising
T 06	Conducting with a score
T 07	Conducting getting louder
T 08	Inventing vocal ostinatos
T 09	Dividing a class into groups
T 10	Conducting start and stop
T 11	Building layers of sound
T 12	Playing a drone accompaniment
T 13	Recognising a word rhythm
T 14	Allocating accompaniment instruments
T 15	Conducting instrumental groups
T 16	Helping to perform a steady beat
T 17	Putting instruments away

Musical independence

Painting with sound (Unit 13) is a more open-ended unit that enables the opportunity for more free composition. The tasks are deliberately broad enough to allow for independence of expression as an individual or part of a group.

Tonic Sol-fa

Dragon scales (Unit 12) makes reference to John Curwen's 19th century Tonic Sol-fa teaching methods. The hand signs used are those established by Kodaly. They are a slightly adapted version of Curwen's hand signs and are the ones most in use today.

Music Express does not aim to teach Curwen or Kodaly methods. The inclusion of the hand signs in ***Music Express Year 4*** is an isolated use, intended to give children the experience of another way of demonstrating the pitch movement of a scale and of melodic phrases. *(Spellings of sol-fa names may vary.)*

Ongoing skills

'Ongoing skills' are identified by the QCA scheme of work as those skills which need to be continually developed and revisited. This is in addition to the activities in the six units. The QCA suggests that learning may take place as the opportunity arises throughout the school week, eg in short 5-minute sessions.

Music Express does not include a separate Ongoing skills unit, but addresses the skills throughout its activities. When using ***Music Express*** as a scheme, you will be fulfilling the learning objectives and outcomes of the QCA Ongoing skills unit.

If you teach music in one weekly lesson, as opposed to three shorter lessons, you may like to select activities from ***Music Express*** for supplementary 5-minute activities. By doing this, you will reinforce more regularly the development of the musical skills identified by the QCA.

Extension and future learning

A & C Black website

Music Express provides all the resources you will need for teaching a year of music. We hope, however, that you will use other songs and activities to ring the changes in subsequent years or to link with other National Curriculum subjects.

The website www.acblack.com/musicexpress lists the ***Music Express*** activities that were drawn from or inspired by other A & C Black books, and links to other books that will supplement the activities in ***Music Express.***

Lullaby rhythms

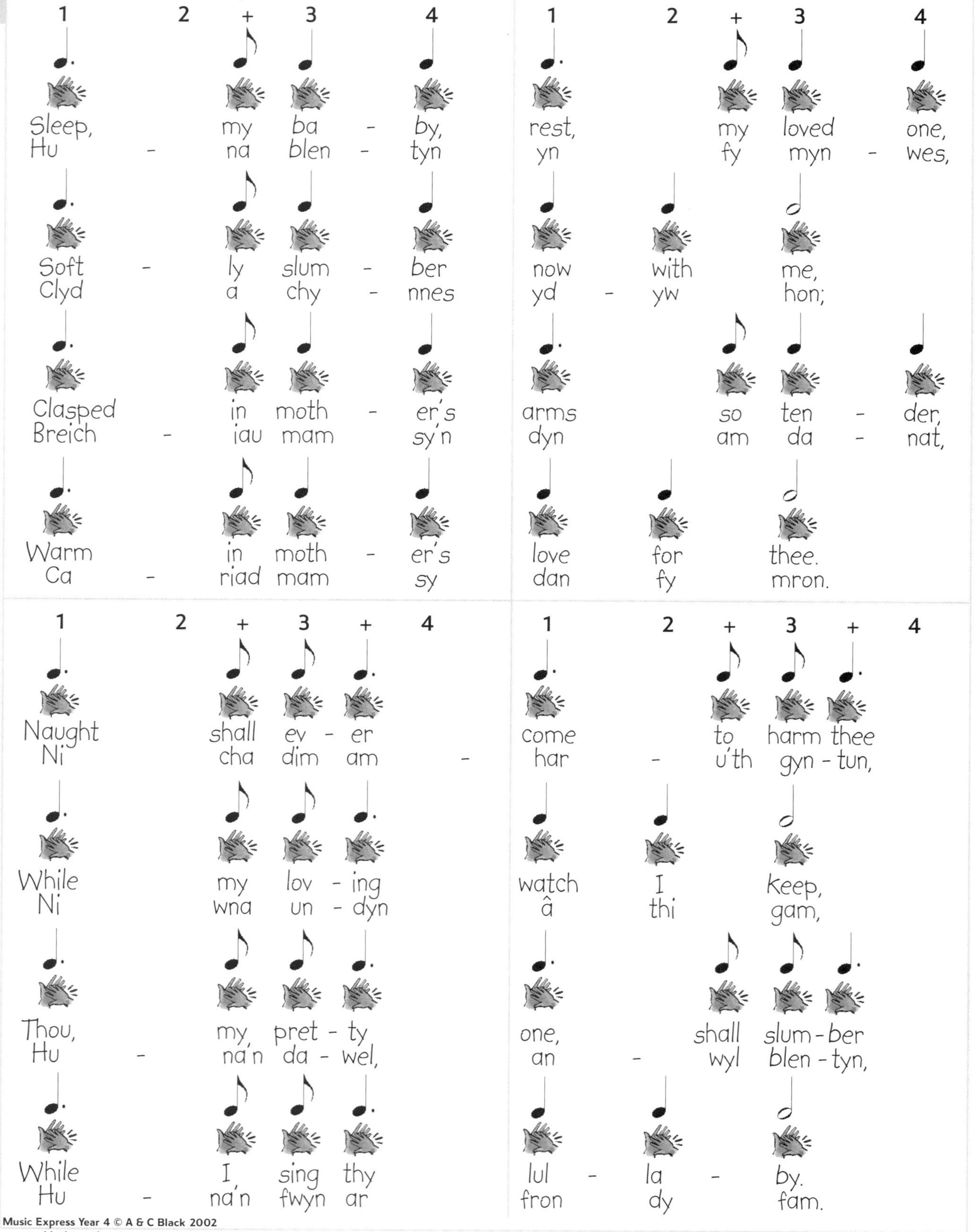

JELLY ON A PLATE

1 Identify phrases in *Jelly on a plate* 13

- Listen to *Jelly on a plate (track 13).* All march on the spot in time to the steady beat.
- Explain that each line of this song is a musical phrase, a section of the melody. Write the words of the song on the board in four lines for the children to see:

1. Jelly on a plate,
2. Jelly on a plate,
3. Wibble, wobble, wibble, wobble,
4. Jelly on a plate.

- All listen again, then clap the rhythm of each line. Ask which lines have exactly the same rhythm. *(Lines 1, 2 and 4.)*
- All sing the song. Concentrate on making the rhythm bouncy.

Teaching tip

- A phrase is a small unit of a melody. A phrase often corresponds to a line of words of a song.

2 Study the notation of *Jelly on a plate* p12 13

- Listen to track 13 again, and all follow the words on the ***Bouncy jelly*** photocopiable. As you listen, point to each syllable in time with the music.
- Ask the children how the music notation represents a bouncy rhythm. *(The notes are spaced in a pattern to match the rhythm of the words. When two syllables are sung close together, the notes are close together and when they are further apart, the notes are further apart.)*
- Explain that the symbol (𝄽) represents a rest *(a silence)*. Demonstrate the effect of the rests by saying 'sh' wherever they occur as you sing. *(You might then repeat the song, putting your finger to your lips instead of saying sh. Sing a third time observing the silence.)*

Background information

- *Jelly on a plate* is a traditional children's rhyme which is often chanted for skipping and other playground games.

3 Combine rhythm patterns from *Jelly on a plate* in an ostinato accompaniment 14

- Listen to more verses of *Jelly on a plate (track 14).* Ask the children how many verses there are. *(Four.)*
- Divide the class into three groups to perform this accompaniment:
  - group 1 marches on the spot in time with the steady beat;
  - group 2 uses untuned wooden percussion instruments to play the rhythm of the words 'jelly on a plate' as an ostinato;
  - group 3 uses scraping and shaking untuned percussion instruments to play the rhythm of the words 'wibble, wobble, wibble, wobble' as an ostinato.
- Practise each ostinato pattern in turn. When everyone is confident, accompany track 14 in the following way:
  - group 1 plays throughout;
  - group 2 joins in at the start of the second verse;
  - group 3 joins in at the start of the third verse;
  - all continue during the fourth verse.

Teaching tip

- Swap parts so that everyone performs each pattern.

Bouncy jelly

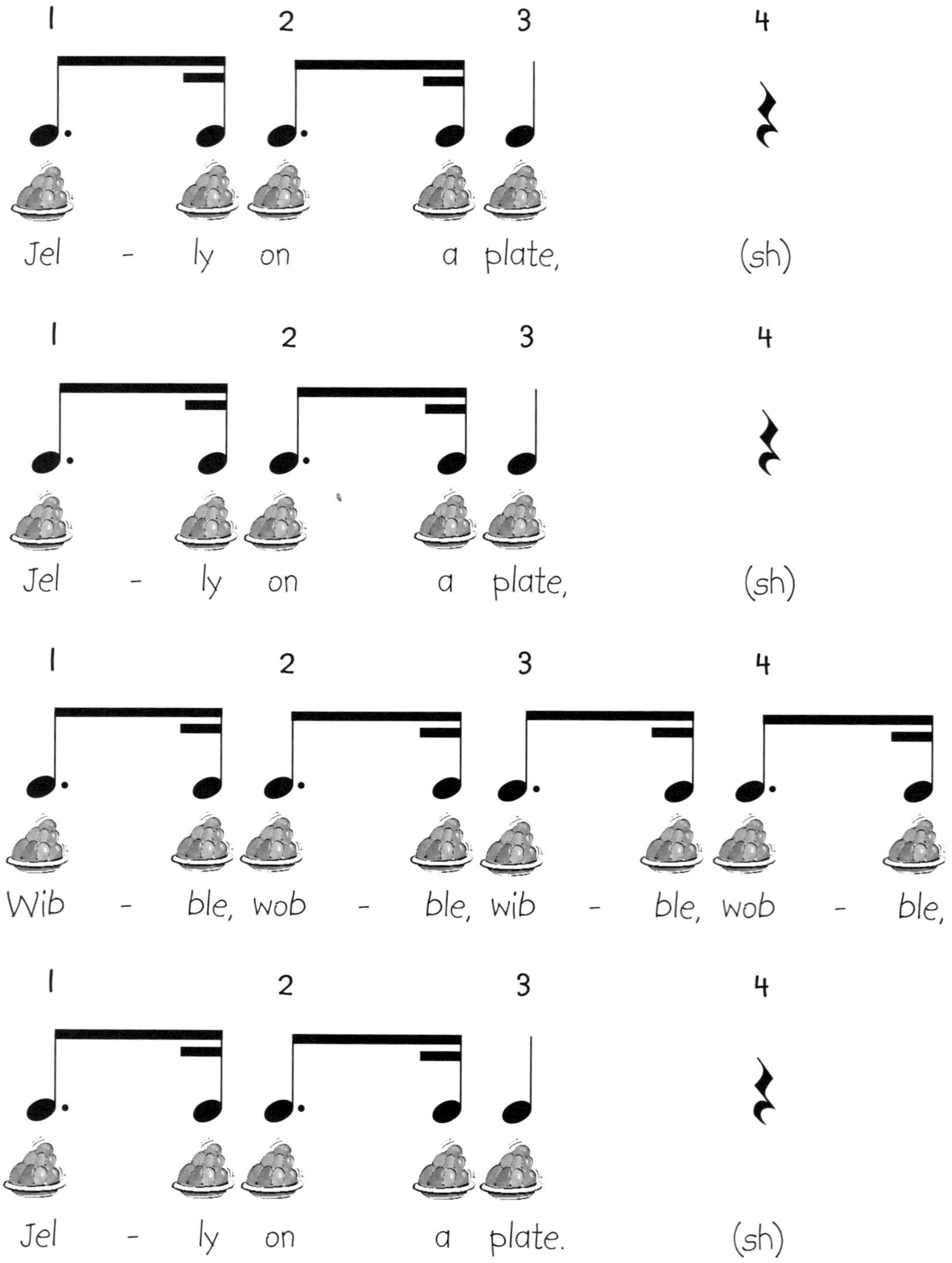

is a rest - in this song it means be silent for one beat

 **- bouncy rhythm**

UNSQUARE RHYTHMS

1 Identify and perform rhythm patterns in *Unsquare dance*

p14 15-17

- Listen to an extract of ***Unsquare dance*** *(track 15)*. Ask the children how many patterns they can hear repeated at the beginning. *(There are two ostinati. One is clapped and the other is played on a double bass.)*
- Listen to track 16, and all follow card 1 on the ***Seven square*** photocopiable. All stamp in time with the double bass three-note pattern.
  (Try this several times until everyone can stamp this pattern in time.)
- Divide the class in half. One half stamps with track 16 following card 1, and the other adds the double clap at the end, as on card 2.
- Listen to track 17. Follow the clapping pattern on card 3. All join in clapping this pattern in time with the CD.
- When everyone is confident, divide the class in half to combine the ostinati: one half performs the stamps and the other half the claps. Then swap over.

Background information

- *Unsquare dance* was composed by Dave Brubeck (1920 -). It demonstrates his experiments in blending complex African rhythms with free improvisation in a jazz style.

Teaching tips

- The music is quite fast so practise this as many times as it takes to give the class support.
- The beat of the piece is in groups of seven. As you perform each ostinato, count the seven beats out loud. Practise slowly and work up to the speed of the CD.
- When combining the ostinati, it may be easier to hear and feel when to play rather than count.

2 Invent two rhythmic ostinati which combine to make seven beats

p14

- When everyone can confidently perform ***Unsquare dance***, divide the class into pairs.
- Each pair uses card 4 on the ***Seven square*** photocopiable and invents two ostinati of their own to perform using body percussion sounds.
- They draw a square round the beats of their first ostinato and a circle round the others to make their second ostinato. Remind each pair to make a note of the body percussion to be used for each ostinato, eg

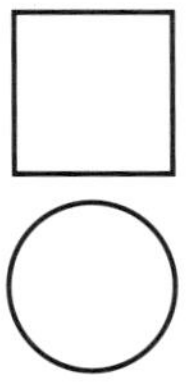

= tap knees

= click fingers

3 Perform the invented rhythm patterns to a backing track

18

- Invite pairs to perform their ostinati to a backing track. Listen to the track first and give each pair time to practise performing their ostinati in time with the beat.
- Each pair performs their ostinati.
- Invite pairs to teach their pattern to the class and all join in playing their ostinati in time with the backing track.

Track
- 19

- Words ⇒ listen
- Read out ⇒ learn by ear
- 10 groups.

1

1

2

1 2 3 4 5 (6) (7)

3

[1] (2) [3] (4) [5] (6) (7)

4

1 2 3 4 5 6 7

To play our ostinati:

□ =

○ =

HIP HOPPY KID

1 Listen to the poem *I'm a hip hoppy kid* performed as a rap 19-20

- Listen to *I'm a hip hoppy kid (track 19)* performed as an energetic rap with a steady beat.

I'm a hip hoppy kid and you'll never catch me nappin,
No matter where I go you'll always hear me rappin ...
I rap to the east and I rap to the west ...
I rap in my socks and I rap in my vest ...
I rap in my sleep and drive the neighbours potty ...
I rap in the bathroom when I'm drying off my botty ...
I rap to the birds and I rap to the bees ...
And when I go completely daft I rap to the trees ...
I can even rap on wheels, I really am the master ...
I wish I'd seen that manhole then I wouldn't be in plaster ...

- Discuss what the poem is about. Where and when did the hip hoppy kid rap? *(In the east, in his socks, in his sleep ...)*
- Listen to a performance of the rap in which the beats are counted *(track 20)*. All perform this body percussion pattern in time to the rap:

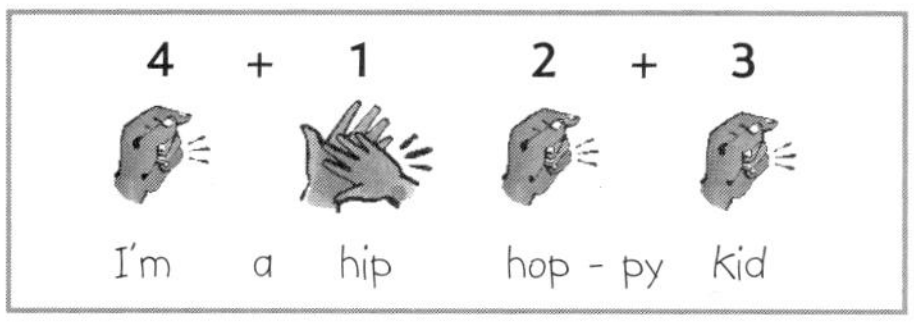

2 Work out the words of *I'm a hip hoppy kid* by ear and identify rhythmic phrases 19 21-22

- Divide the class into ten groups, one for each line of the rap. All listen again *(track 19)* and each group writes down their allocated line of the poem. *(You may need to listen to the poem several times for each group to write their line down correctly.)*
- When each group has completed their line, all perform the rap to the backing track *(track 21)*. Each group takes a turn to rap their line.
- Copy the following two patterns onto the board:

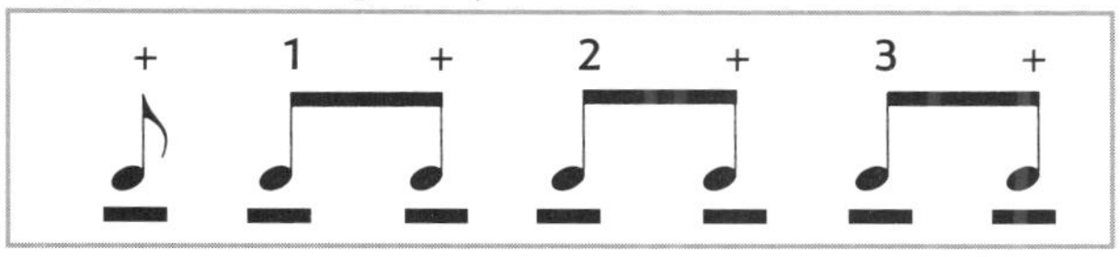

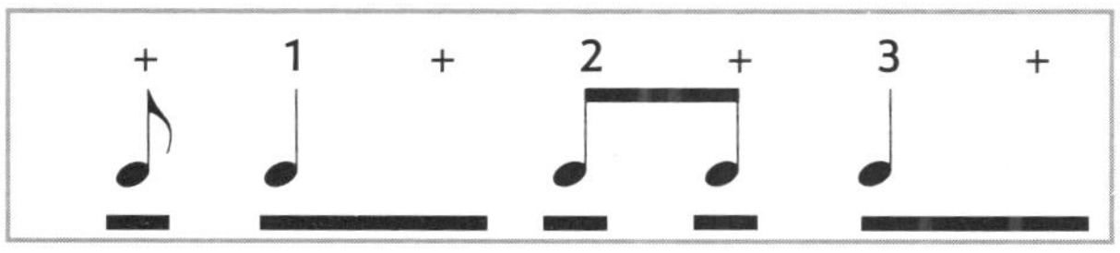

All clap each pattern with track 22, then ask the class to work out which pattern matches the second part of each line of the poem. *(The first pattern matches lines 1, 2, 5, 6, 9 and 10, eg 'you'll never catch me nappin', and the second pattern matches lines 3, 4, 7 and 8, eg 'I rap to the west'.)*

- Perform the rap again, all clapping the rhythm pattern of the second part of each line of the poem.

3 Invent lyrics for a *Clean school rap* using the structure of *I'm a hip hoppy kid*

p16

- Explain that the class is going to write a ***Clean school rap*** using the rhythms of ***I'm a hip hoppy kid.***
- The ten groups from activity 2 each invent a line about keeping the school clean. The words must fit the rhythm pattern of their allocated line in activity 2, eg to fit the first line *('I'm a hip hoppy kid and you'll never catch me nappin')*:

We've a clean happy school and we all work hard to keep it

- Work together as a class to help each group invent their line and make the rap flow well from one group to the next. Write down the finished rap on the ***Clean school rap*** photocopiable.

Clean school rap

Write down the class *Clean school rap*:

KEEP OUR SCHOOL CLEAN AND TIDY!

1 Perform the *Clean school rap* with body percussion accompaniment

p16 21

- Rehearse the ***Clean school rap*** with the backing track *(track 21).* All perform the body percussion ostinato *(from lesson 5, activity 1)* and each group takes it in turn to rap their line.
- When everyone can confidently perform their line of the rap with the backing track, try without the CD. Decide whether you prefer the rap with or without the backing track.
- Make a recording of the class performing their ***Clean school rap*** with the body percussion accompaniment.

Teaching tips

- You will need the completed *Clean school rap* photocopiable from last lesson to revise your lyrics.
- Some children may like to invent a new body percussion ostinato to perform with the rap.

2 Invent movement to accompany the rap and decide a structure for a class performance

21

- Divide the class into pairs. Each pair invents one or two movements to perform in time to the rap.
  (Encourage the children to think of strong rhythmic movements that are easily repeatable. They may be whole body dance movements or simple actions using only hands or feet.)
- Each pair performs their movements to the rest of the class.
- Perform the ***Clean school rap*** as a class, adding some of the movements. Consider which movements are the most effective, and which work well together.
- Perform the rap several times, trying out different performance ideas. Encourage the children to be as imaginative as possible. Consider:
  - rapping different lines at the same time, or having two performance groups starting the rap at different times;
  - breaking the rap into small sections with the movement in between;
  - whether to use the backing track or not.

  Decide who will perform what and when, and where everyone will stand for the performance.

Teaching tip

- Try to ensure that everyone is involved in rehearsing and developing the rap, by playing and by contributing ideas.

3 Rehearse then perform the accompanied version of the *Clean school rap*

- Rehearse the ***Clean school rap*** in the structure decided in activity 2.
- Perform the class composition to a friendly audience and record the performance on audio or video cassette.
- Listen to and discuss the performance. Consider:
  - whether the performance was well coordinated;
  - whether the performance had expression, for example variations of loud and quiet voices to reflect the meaning of the words.

RHYTHMIC ACCOMPANIMENTS

1 Listen to ostinato rhythm patterns in the accompaniment of three songs

23-25

- All listen to **Freedom** *(track 23)*. Ask the children how the voices are accompanied.
  (First time: one voice unaccompanied; second time: two voices with a drum playing a steady beat throughout; third time: three voices with the drum playing a repeated rhythm pattern.)
- Listen again, and all join in tapping the drum part using fingertips on knees.
- Listen to ***Ki yo wah ji neh*** *(track 24)*. As you listen, all tap the tambourine's steady beat using the fingertips of the left hand on the left knee, and the drum's steady beat using the fingertips of the right hand on the right knee.
  (If this is too hard, tap them separately.)
- Listen again, and ask what other sound can be heard throughout.
  (There is a sound effect for the wind. This adds colour and reminds us of the context.)
- Listen to **Sambalele** *(track 25)*. Ask the children to describe the accompaniment.
  (Maracas play a steady beat and claves and a drum play repeated patterns throughout.)
- Listen again, and encourage the children to invent another rhythm pattern to add to the accompaniment using fingertips on knees.

Teaching tips

- Accompaniments can be sung or played, and feature in music throughout the world.
- They can be musically simple or elaborate and their purpose is to help enrich and express the meaning of the song.

Background information

- *Freedom* is a traditional Caribbean song for all people throughout the world who are suffering through war or neglect.
- *Ki yo wah ji neh* is a Native American song that describes a hunter trying to paddle his canoe against the wind.
- *Sambalele* is a Brazilian song describing a mischievous monkey who has a sore head after feasting on stolen food!
- *Did the rum do?* is an Irish folk song.
- The bodhran is an Irish hand drum, played using a double-headed beater. It is used to accompany many styles of Celtic dance music.

2 Compare three different accompaniments to the song *Did the rum do?*

26

- Listen to *Did the rum do? (track 26)*. Ask the children how each of the three performances differ.
  (First time: sung with an accordion accompaniment; second time: sung faster with a bodhran drum accompanying; third time: melody played very fast on penny whistle as the bodhran accompanies.)
- Invite individuals to suggest a combination of voice and instrument that might be used if the song was performed a fourth time.
  (Explain that there is no right answer, you are just asking for suggestions.)

bodhran – front and back

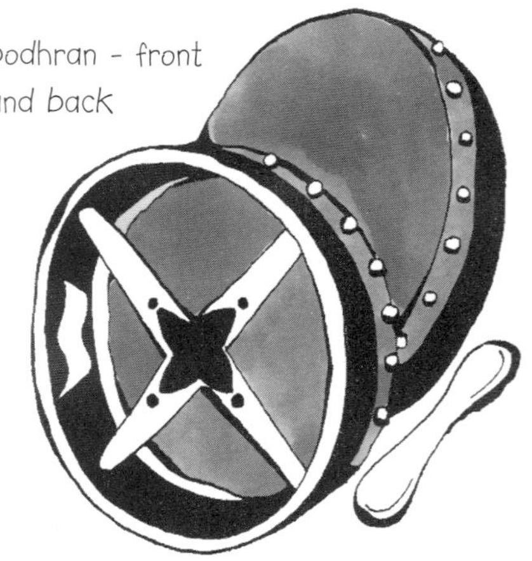

3 Choose a favourite accompaniment and join in with the rhythm patterns

23-26

- Listen again to the songs heard this lesson, and join in with any or all of the accompaniments.
  (Some children may like to use untuned percussion instruments rather than just tapping knees.)
- Encourage the children to say which song and accompaniment they preferred, indicating their reasons.
- If there is an overall class favourite, play the track again and all join in with the song and the accompaniment.

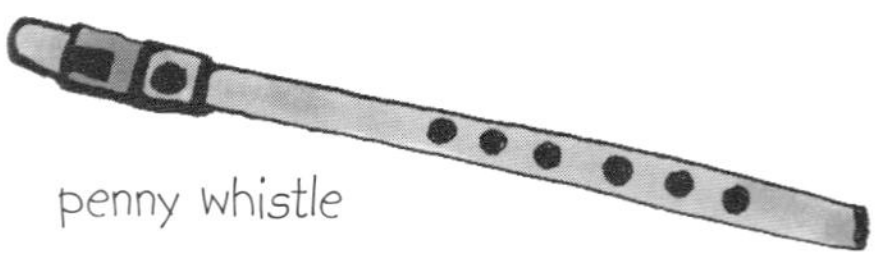

penny whistle

KI YO WAH JI NEH

1 Identify melodic phrases in *Ki yo wah ji neh*

24 27-28

- Listen to *Ki yo wah ji neh (track 24).*
- Explain that each line of the song is a musical phrase - a section of the melody. Listen to track 27, which indicates when each of the four phrases starts. Mark them together by tracing an arc in the air for each phrase.
- Ask whether any of the phrases have the same melody. *(Phrases 2 and 4 are the same: 'Ki yo wah ji neh, ki yo wah ji neh'.)*

  Listen to phrases 2 and 4 played on their own *(track 28)* to confirm this.
- Listen again to track 28 and copy the phrase immediately, singing it to lah.

Teaching tips

- A phrase is a small unit of a melody. It often corresponds to a line of a song.
- Melodies have a natural ebb and flow because of this phrase structure.

2 Play some phrases of *Ki yo wah ji neh* by ear

p20 28

- Listen again to the phrase 'Ki yo wah ji neh, ki yo wah ji neh' *(track 28).* The children trace the pitch movement with their hands as they sing. *(As the pitch goes higher and lower, their hands should get higher and lower to match.)*
- Invite an individual to play the phrase by ear on tuned percussion - notes C D E F G A - starting on the note F. Invite the rest of the class to help by showing the pitch movement with their hands.
- Check the notes of the phrase as a class. As you play each note, ask the children to say whether the next note is the same, higher or lower. When all are agreed, the children write the note names on the ***Playing by ear*** photocopiable.

Answer:

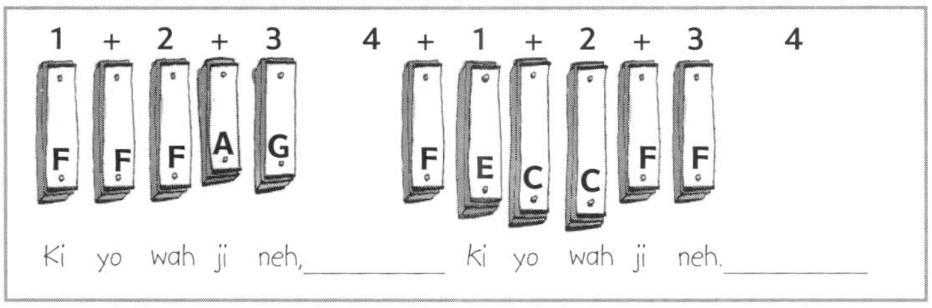

Teaching tips

- Encourage as many children as possible to try playing the phrase by ear.
- Children may like to bring in instruments from home for this activity.

3 Perform the *Ki yo wah ji neh* phrases as part of the song

p20 24

- Small groups of tuned percussion players rehearse playing the phrase 'Ki yo wah ji neh, ki yo wah ji neh' to track 24. *(The song is sung three times, so the phrase will be played six times in all. Different groups of children might play the phrase each time it occurs.)*
- Perform the song with the CD like this:
  - tuned percussion groups: play the phrase 'Ki yo wah ji neh, ki yo wah ji neh' each time it occurs;
  - singing group: join in singing the phrase 'Ki yo wah ji neh, ki yo wah ji neh' and mime strong paddling actions to the beat;
  - percussion group: play the tambourine and drum beats indicated on the photocopiable.

Playing by ear

Work out the melody of the phrase using these notes:

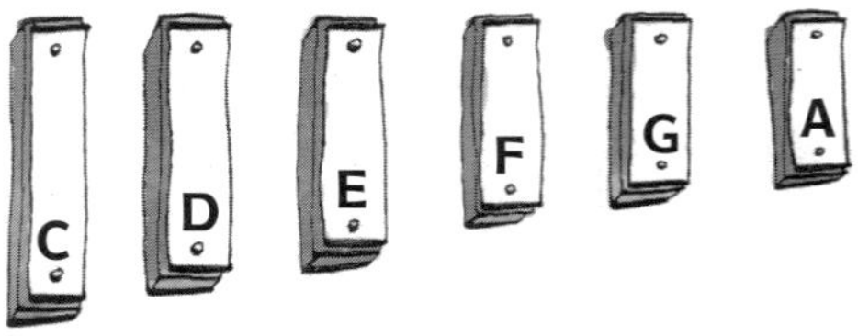

1 + 2 + 3 + 4 + 1 + 2 + 3 + 4 +

F

Ki yo wah ji neh,____________ Ki yo wah ji neh.____________

Ki yo wah ji neh **percussion accompaniment:**

1 + 2 + 3 + 4 + 1 + 2 + 3 + 4 +

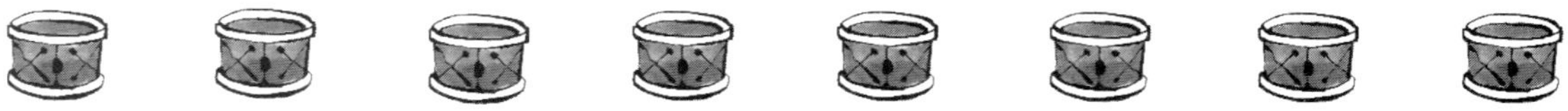

Ki yo wah ji neh,____________ Ki yo wah ji neh.____________

CHRISTMAS CALYPSO

1 Introduce the song *Christmas calypso*

- Listen to the whole song, *Christmas calypso (track 29)*. Then teach the chorus:

First section:
So let the bells all ring,
Children sing, it's time for a holiday;
Let's all jump and shout,
Ev'ryone come out and sing!

Second section:
So let the bells all ring,
Children sing, it's time for a holiday;
Let's all jump for joy,
Ev'ry girl and boy bringing gladness.

- Listen to the song again, and all join in with the chorus.

Teaching tips

- Write the words onto the board. All say the words out loud together first, then teach the melody.
- When learning the chorus, use musical games to help, eg
  - divide the class into four groups, each group sings one section of the chorus with the recording;
  - sing one line of the chorus out loud and sing the next line in your heads;
  - start singing the song in your head. Turn down the CD volume and keep singing the chorus in your heads, turn it back up again and all join in. Are you all in the same place?

2 Identify melodic phrases in the chorus of *Christmas calypso*

- All sing the chorus of *Christmas calypso* with track 29. Ask the children how many phrases there are in each section of the chorus. Encourage the children to find the phrases by tracing an arc in the air as they sing. They may also find it helpful to think about where they breathe.
  (There are four phrases in each section. Each line of the chorus is a phrase.)
- Listen to track 30 which divides each section of the chorus into four phrases. As you listen, all stand up at the start of the first phrase and sit down at the start of the second, and so on.
  (The start of each phrase is indicated on the CD track.)
- All sing along with track 30, breathing at the end of each phrase *(as long as it feels comfortable)*. Trace an arc in the air as you sing each phrase.

3 Learn the verses of *Christmas calypso*

- Teach the verses of the song using track 29.

V1 Sing it on the hillside, sing on the mountains,
Christmas Day is almost here!
Sing it round the valleys, forests and fountains,
Christmas Day is near!

V2 Decorate the house with tinsel and berry,
Christmas Day is almost here!
This'll be the time to give and be merry,
Christmas Day is near!

- Ask how many phrases there are in each verse. *(The children may suggest two longer phrases or four shorter ones.)* Listen to track 31 to hear the difference. The first time, the verse is sung in two phrases, the second time, in four. Notice that the performance is smoother when sung in only two phrases.
- All sing the song all the way through. Trace an arc in the air for each phrase to help the children feel the natural ebb and flow of the song as they sing.

Teaching tips

- Write the words on the board to help the children learn the verses.
- Record the class singing at different stages throughout the lesson to hear how they improve.

RHYTHMS AND JIVES

1 Add a steady beat to *Christmas calypso* 32

- All sing the first verse and chorus of *Christmas calypso* with track 32.
- Invite members of the class to add a steady beat using body percussion or untuned instruments. Encourage the children to investigate playing different beats with the song, eg

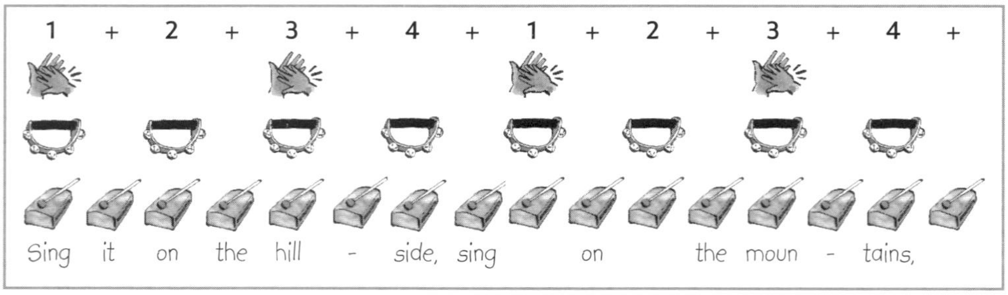

Play the CD track several times to enable the children to try out their ideas, eg

- use different instruments for the verse and for the chorus;
- play different beats for the verse and chorus;
- play a percussion instrument such as an Indian bell on the first note of every phrase;
- include a hand jive in time to a beat for the verse or chorus or both.

Jive 1
With one hand above the other and palms facing downwards, slide hands over and under each other in time to the beat.

Jive 2
Tap one fist on top of the other in time to the beat. Alternate hands.

Jive 3
Draw a circle in the air in time to the beat using the index finger. Alternate hands.

2 Add repeated rhythm patterns to *Christmas calypso* 29

- Invite a volunteer to choose some words from the song to tap as a rhythm pattern on untuned percussion through all or part of it, eg 'sing it on the hill' or 'ev'ry girl and boy'.
(Encourage the children to choose interesting rhythms.)

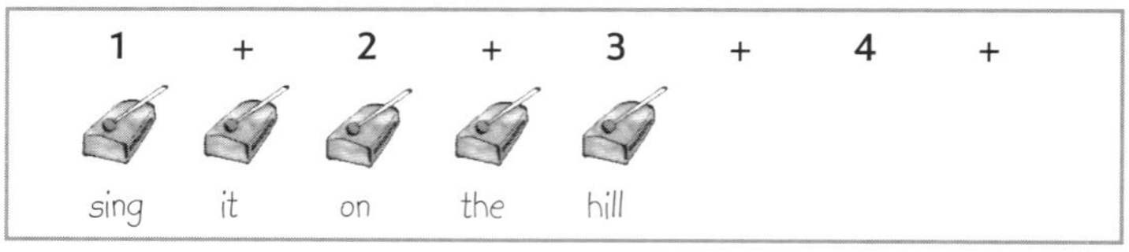

- Encourage individuals to invent more rhythm patterns that go well with the song but are not necessarily created from the words.
- Listen again to the CD track, and take turns tapping each invented rhythm using body or untuned percussion.

Background information

- The rhythm of the words 'ev'ry girl and boy' is a traditional calypso rhythm.

3 Combine rhythm patterns and beat in *Christmas calypso* 29

- Using the CD track for support, develop the class arrangement of the song. Decide together when the different beats and rhythm patterns from activities 1 and 2 should occur in the song, and on what instruments. Consider when to include hand jives.
- Rehearse the class arrangement.
(Make sure the accompaniment does not overpower the singing.)

PLAYING CHRISTMAS CALYPSO

1 Learn to play a phrase from *Christmas calypso* by ear

p24 33-34

- Divide the class into small groups. Give each a **Calypso melody** photocopiable and a set of tuned percussion with the notes indicated.
- Explain that each group is to work out how to play one of the two phrases from the first verse by ear. The starting note is given.
- Play the two phrases *(tracks 33 and 34)* at regular intervals so the groups may hear the notes and check their own progress.
- When the groups can play their phrase by ear they write it on the photocopiable. Encourage them to work the notes out one at a time.

Phrase 1:

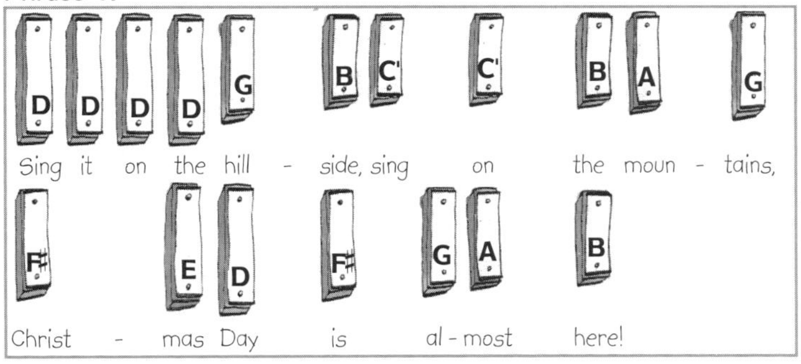

Phrase 2:

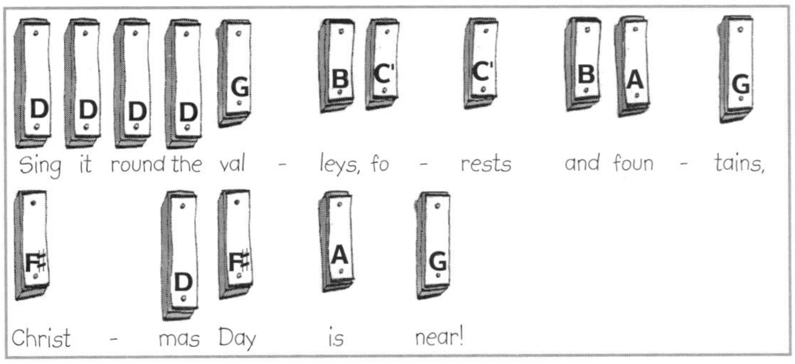

3 Consider the intention of *Christmas calypso* and develop a performance style to suit the song

29

- Ask the children what the purpose and mood of this song is. *(It is a song to celebrate Christmas. It is joyous and bright.)*

  Ask how this should affect the performance. *(The singing and playing should sound happy and bright. Everyone should smile and enjoy performing.)*
- Discuss ways of adding expression and contrast to the singing, eg
  - decide which parts of the song will be sung loudly, and which quietly;
  - discuss whether the change from loud to quiet will be gradual or sudden.
- Try performing the song in different ways and decide as a class which is the most effective.
- Rehearse the singing. If necessary, appoint a conductor to signal when to sing loudly and quietly.
- Invite groups of children to take turns watching the rest of the class perform. The listeners give feedback on: expression; whether the words are clear; whether the children look and sound joyous and bright.

Teaching tips

- Use any available tuned instruments and encourage children to bring in instruments from home for this activity.
- Encourage groups to work carefully together as a team to complete their task.
- To work out the pitch, the children should ask whether each note is the same, higher or lower than the previous one. If it is higher or lower, they need to consider by how much.

2 Rehearse playing the *Christmas calypso* phrases in time with the CD

p24 35

- Each group rehearses their phrase in time with track 35. Play the track several times to give practice at keeping in time, and to enable different members of the group to play.

Calypso melody

Work out the melody of either of these two phrases using these notes:

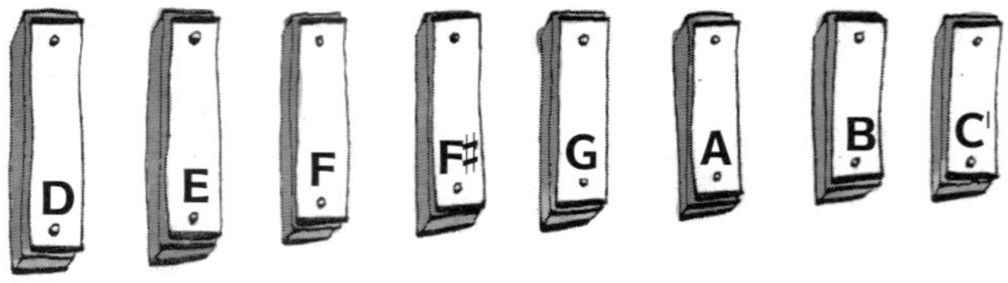

Phrase 1

1 + 2 + 3 + 4 + 1 + 2 + 3 + 4 +

D

1 + 2 + 3 + 4 + 1 + 2 + 3 + 4 +

Phrase 2

1 + 2 + 3 + 4 + 1 + 2 + 3 + 4 +

D

1 + 2 + 3 + 4 + 1 + 2 + 3 + 4 +

COMPLETELY CALYPSO

1 Complete the class arrangement of *Christmas calypso* 36

- Plan a class performance of *Christmas calypso* using the backing track if required *(track 36)*. The performance should include:
  - both verses and choruses, sung expressively;
  - rhythm patterns and steady beats performed on untuned percussion;
  - the melody of the verse played on tuned percussion or children's own instruments.

  As a class decide which rhythm patterns and beats to perform at which points in the song *(as discussed in the fourth lesson, p22).*
- Write the structure of your performance on the board, eg

Verse 1	all sing
Chorus 1	first section: add untuned percussion playing beats and rhythm patterns second section: different instruments play beats and rhythm patterns
Verse 1 repeat	add tuned percussion instruments playing the melody
Interlude	
Verse 2	untuned percussion beats and rhythm patterns
Chorus 2	as chorus 1
Verse 2 repeat	singers divide in half: one half sings the first phrase and the other half the second phrase
Last phrase	all sing

Teaching tips

- Use this lesson to rehearse the work all the way through before presenting it to an audience.
- Make a note of the class decisions about where everyone will stand for the performance.
- Use the CD backing track to support as much as you want.
- Make sure everyone is aware of what they are doing and in which order.
- If possible, include some hand jives, they will liven the performance and give it a more joyous feel.

2 Plan and rehearse the class arrangement of *Christmas calypso* 36

- As a class, plan the performance. Consider:
  - where you will perform;
  - how everyone will enter and leave the performance area;
  - whether everyone will stand or sit;
  - whether the instrumentalists need written music or can play their parts from memory;
  - whether to appoint a conductor;
  - whether anyone will announce the piece or talk about the arrangement before you start.
- Rehearse the performance. Remind the class to smile and enjoy it. If you can, record the final rehearsal and evaluate it as a class before performing in front of others. Consider:
  - whether everyone played and sang in time together;
  - if you performed without the backing track, whether the song became too fast or slow;
  - whether the expression was effective;
  - whether the words were clear;
  - whether the performance captured the spirit of the song;
  - whether it would be useful to appoint a conductor if you had not already.

3 Perform *Christmas calypso* to an audience

- Perform the class arrangement of the song to a friendly audience.

PITCH MOVEMENT

1 Follow the pitch movement of the melody in the song *Jibber jabber* (37)

- Listen to *Jibber jabber*. Ask the children which instrument is playing the melody. *(The piano.)*
- Ask the children to describe the mood of the melody.
  (It is bouncy and cheerful. It makes you feel like moving.)
- Listen again and all follow the pitch movement of the melody by raising and lowering your hands to match.
  (You might like to repeat this activity a few times for the children to become familiar with the tune.)

- Ask the children to follow the pitch of the melody with their hands again, but this time to concentrate on moving their hands more precisely. Match small and large pitch movements with correspondingly small and large hand movements.
- Ask what the children noticed about the pitch of the melody.
  (Some of the notes of the melody are far apart and others are close together.)

Teaching tips

- Pitch refers to the complete range of sounds in music from the lowest to the highest.
- The notes of a melody may move up or down in small steps or larger leaps, or stay on the same note.
- The distance between two notes is called an interval.
- When working out how to draw the pitch movement of the melody on the board, ask the children to consider:
  - whether the melody is moving up or down;
  - how far apart notes are in relation to others;
  - whether two intervals are the same or different.
- You may need to listen to the track several times to work out each pitch.

2 Identify leaps in a melody by ear (38-39)

- Listen to track 38 a few times. All follow the pitch movement of the melody as precisely as possible with your hands.
- Invite volunteers to represent the pitch movement of the first three leaps in a diagram on the board, eg in dot notation:

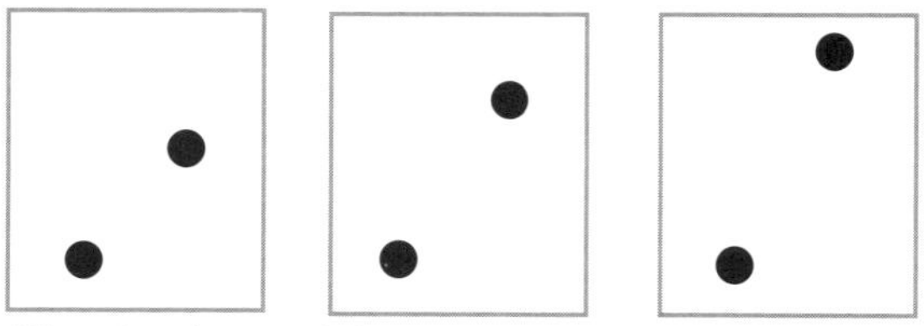

- All notice that each leap starts from the same note and leaps higher each time.
- Invite individuals to work out the pitch of these leaps on chime bars. The first note is D. Answer:

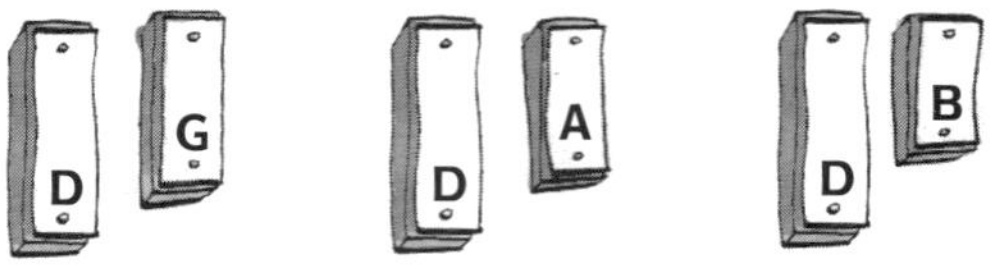

- Listen to track 38 again, and challenge individuals to work out the pitch of the second set of leaps. Answer:

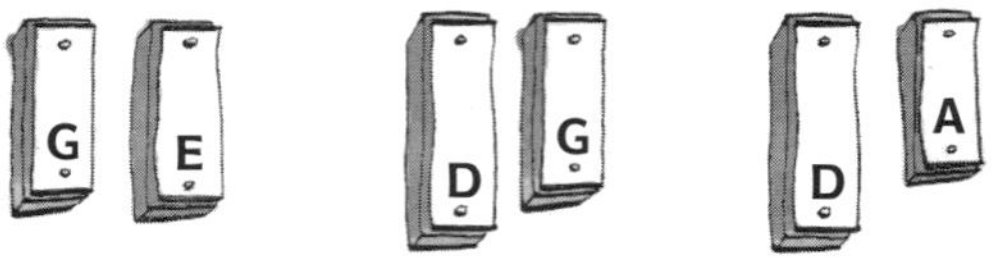

- Play and sing along with track 39 in which the names of the notes of the leaps are sung.

3 Demonstrate leaps in a melody using whole body movement (40)

- Listen to *Gavotte (track 40)*. Ask the children to count how many times the melody leaps up then down again. *(Five.)*
- Listen again and all stand up and sit down when the melody leaps up then down.

PITCH YOUR MELODY

1 Work out melodic intervals in *Simple melody* by ear

41-42

- Listen to ***Simple melody*** *(track 41)* and all follow the pitch movement of the melody with hands. Ask the children whether the melody moves by step or by leap. *(By leap.)*
- Invite volunteers to work out by ear the first three rising leaps on tuned percussion - notes A, B, C D E F G A, starting from the note A,. *Answer:*

- Invite volunteers to work out by ear the three falling leaps of the second phrase, starting from the note high A. *Answer:*

- Play track 41 several times for the children to perform these two sets of leaps with the CD.
- Listen to track 42 and ask the children to identify how the melody is different from track 41. *(An extra note has been added between the notes of the last interval on each line. The notes now move by step.)*

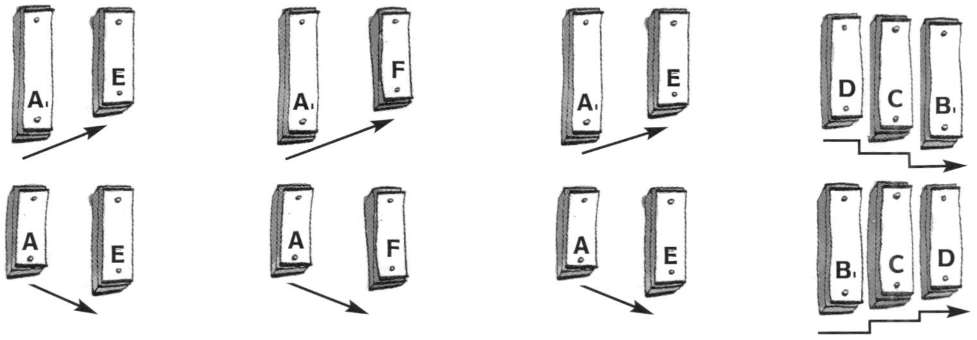

2 Invent melodies from a set of intervals

p28 41

- Listen to ***Simple melody*** again *(track 41)* and all follow the melody on the ***Playing intervals*** photocopiable. Notice that the melody is made up of eight pairs of intervals.
- The children create their own melodies by rearranging the intervals. The rules are that the order of the shapes has to stay the same, but the children can choose which colour shape to play in each position.

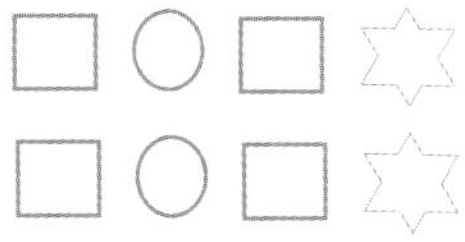

Demonstrate the activity by playing the example on the photocopiable.

Teaching tip

- You may prefer the class to divide into pairs or groups or stay as a whole, depending on the tuned percussion resources available.

3 Perform and record the new melodies

43

- Perform the new melodies with the backing track. *(Record these performances if you can.)*
- Appraise each performance with the class. Ask how each melody was invented, and discuss whether the melody was played in time with the backing track.

Playing intervals

Simple melody

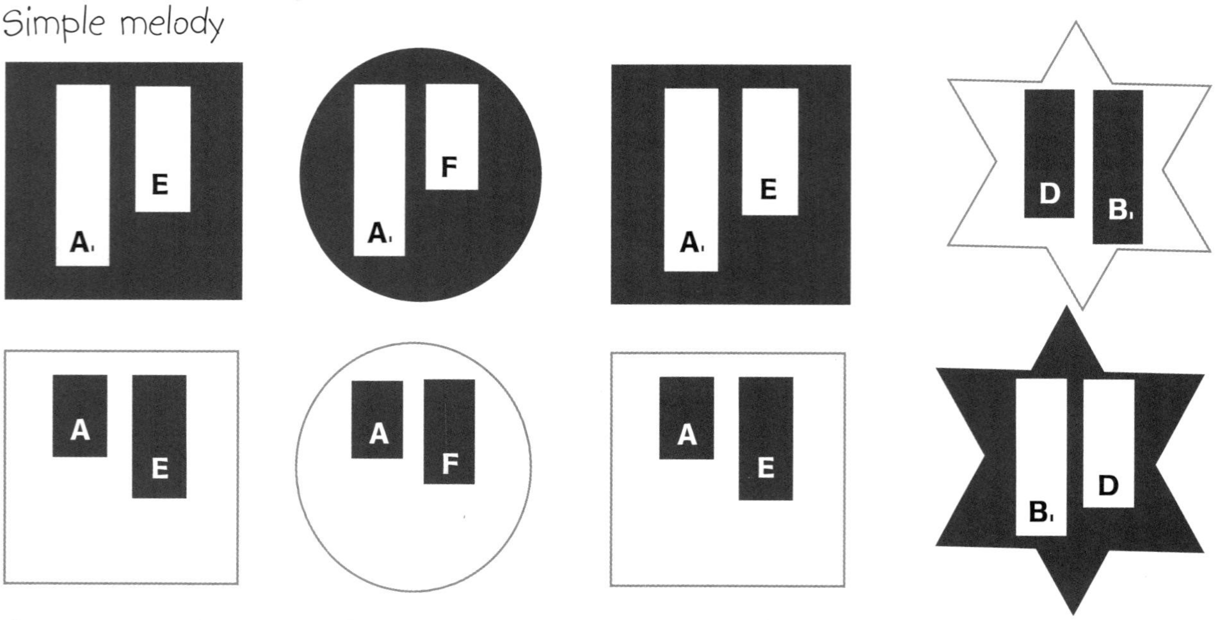

Rearrange the intervals to create your own simple melody. Remember, the shapes must stay in the same order.

Example:

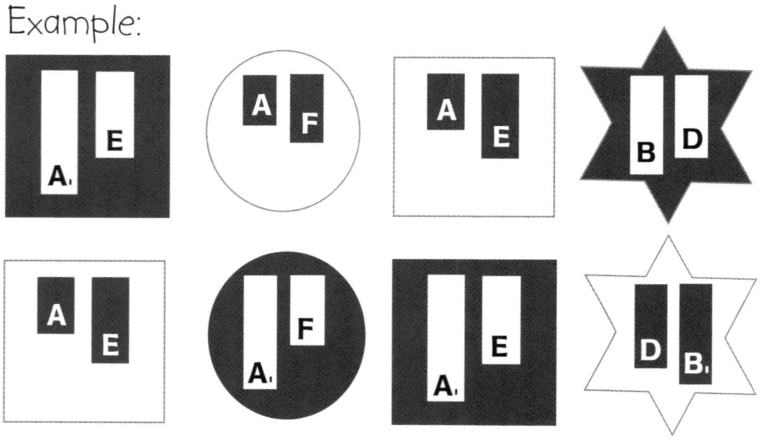

Invent your own melody:

SKYE BOAT SONG

1 Learn *Skye boat song* and discuss the phrases

44

- Listen to ***Skye boat song*** *(track 44)*. Tell the children what the song is about. *(Bonnie Prince Charlie escaping to the Isle of Skye.)*
- Ask how many sections the song has. *(Three: chorus, verse, chorus.)*
- Teach the song.

Ch 'Speed, bonnie boat, like a bird on the wing,
Onward,' the sailors cry.
'Carry the lad that's born to be king
Over the sea to Skye.'

Vs Loud the winds howl, loud the waves roar,
Thunder clouds rend the air;
Baffled, our foes stand on the shore,
Follow they will not dare.

Ch 'Speed, bonnie boat, like a bird on the wing, ...

- Ask the children where the phrases begin and end in this song. *(At the end of each line of the lyrics.)* Sing the song, all demonstrating the phrases by tracing an arc in the air.
- Ask the children which melodic phrases are the same. *(The first and third line of the chorus; the second and fourth line of the chorus; the first and third line of the verse; the second and fourth line of the verse.)*

Background information

- After the battle of Culloden in 1746, Bonnie Prince Charlie fled west with a ransom on his head. Flora Macdonald disguised the prince as her maid to escape by boat to the Isle of Skye from where he then escaped to France.

2 Learn to play the melody of the verse by ear

45

- Listen to the verse of ***Skye boat song*** *(track 45)*, and all show the pitch movement of the melody in the air with hands.
- As a class, work out the melody of the verse using tuned percussion - notes E G A and B. The melody starts on the note B. *(Answer:)*

- Sing the verse with track 45, with a group playing the melody.

Teaching tips

- To work out the notes of a melody by ear, listen carefully to the intervals between the notes:
  - is the next note higher, lower or the same?
  - is there a big leap or do the notes move by step?
- Encourage the children to sing the melody quietly or play the CD track several times.

3 Record a performance of *Skye boat song* with groups playing the melody and adding sound effects

44

- Discuss the mood and feeling behind the song *(eg fear, bravery, power of the wind and waves, strength ...)*.
- Invite individuals to suggest vocal and untuned percussion sounds to add to the verse to help capture the mood of the song *(eg a deep drum played getting louder then quieter throughout could represent the storm; a single cymbal crash could represent a lightning flash ...)*.
- Rehearse the song with track 44. One group plays the melody of the verse and another plays the sound effects while the rest sing. Invite individuals to listen and evaluate the balance between the parts, eg whether the sound effects are too loud.
- Record a performance.

SCALY SONGS

1 Identify and learn a scale passage in a melody 46

- Listen to an extract of *You can do it (track 46)*, then teach the chorus.

You can do it,
You can do it,
You can do it if you really try.
You can meet that challenge,
Beat that challenge,
If you really try,
And when you've succeeded you'll feel nine feet high.

- Ask the children where the melody of the chorus descends step by step. *(The last line.)*
- Listen to the song again and all join in singing the chorus. All use hand movements to demonstrate the descending step movement in the last line.
- Invite individuals to play along with the CD on tuned percussion. *(NB the first notes are repeated, but then they move down by step, one note per syllable.)*

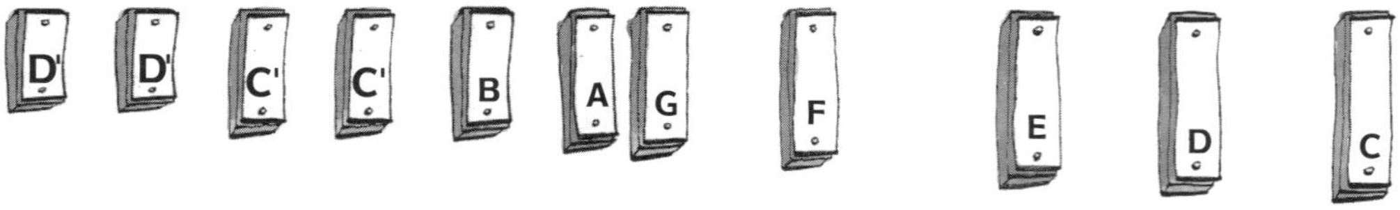

And when you've suc - ceed - ed you'll feel nine______ feet______ high.

Teaching tips

- The word scale is taken from the Latin 'scala' meaning a ladder.
- A scale is the series of notes on which a piece of music is based. This is heard very clearly in *You can do it* and *Do-re-mi* where the scale itself is a feature of the melody.

2 Learn to sing the first melody from *Do-re-mi* and use Kodaly hand signs

p31 47-48

- All listen to the first melody from **Do-re-mi** *(track 47)*, then teach it to the children.

Doe - a deer, a female deer,
Ray - a drop of golden sun.
Me - a name I call myself
Far - a long, long way to run.
Sew - a needle pulling thread,
La - a note to follow sew.
Tea - a drink with jam and bread
That will bring us back to doe.
Do-re-mi-fa-so-la-ti-do. So Do!

- All notice that the first note of each line is one step higher than the previous. Listen to the song again, pointing to the first syllable of each line on the ***Tonic Sol-fa*** photocopiable as it is sung. *(Explain that John Curwen invented a system of notation called 'Tonic Sol-fa'. Each note in the scale is given a note name and a hand sign.)*
- Ask how the songwriter helped us to remember the names of the Tonic Sol-fa. *(By giving a 'sounds like' definition for each name.)*
- Learn the Tonic Sol-fa names using the photocopiable and track 48. Practise singing the scale with the CD and making the hand sign for each note. *(The hand moves higher as the notes get higher.)*
- All join in singing the first melody from **Do-re-mi** *(track 47)*, making the hand signs for the first syllable of each line.

Background information

- A method of using syllables to name notes was invented by Guido of Arezzo (c991 – c1033). The syllables he used are the first of each of the opening lines of a hymn to St John.
- Syllables were used 900 years later by John Curwen in his method of teaching sight singing called *Tonic Sol-fa*, a reliable method still in use. Curwen gave each syllable a hand sign and in the 1930s Kodaly, the Hungarian composer, refined the hand signs to the ones most used today.

(See introduction, p7)

3 Learn the second melody from *Do-re-mi*

p32 49

- Teach the second melody from ***Do-re-mi*** *(track 49)* using the ***Prompt sheet*** photocopiable, and the hand signs.

Soh doh lah fah me doh ray,
Soh doh lah te doh ray doh.

Tonic Sol-fa

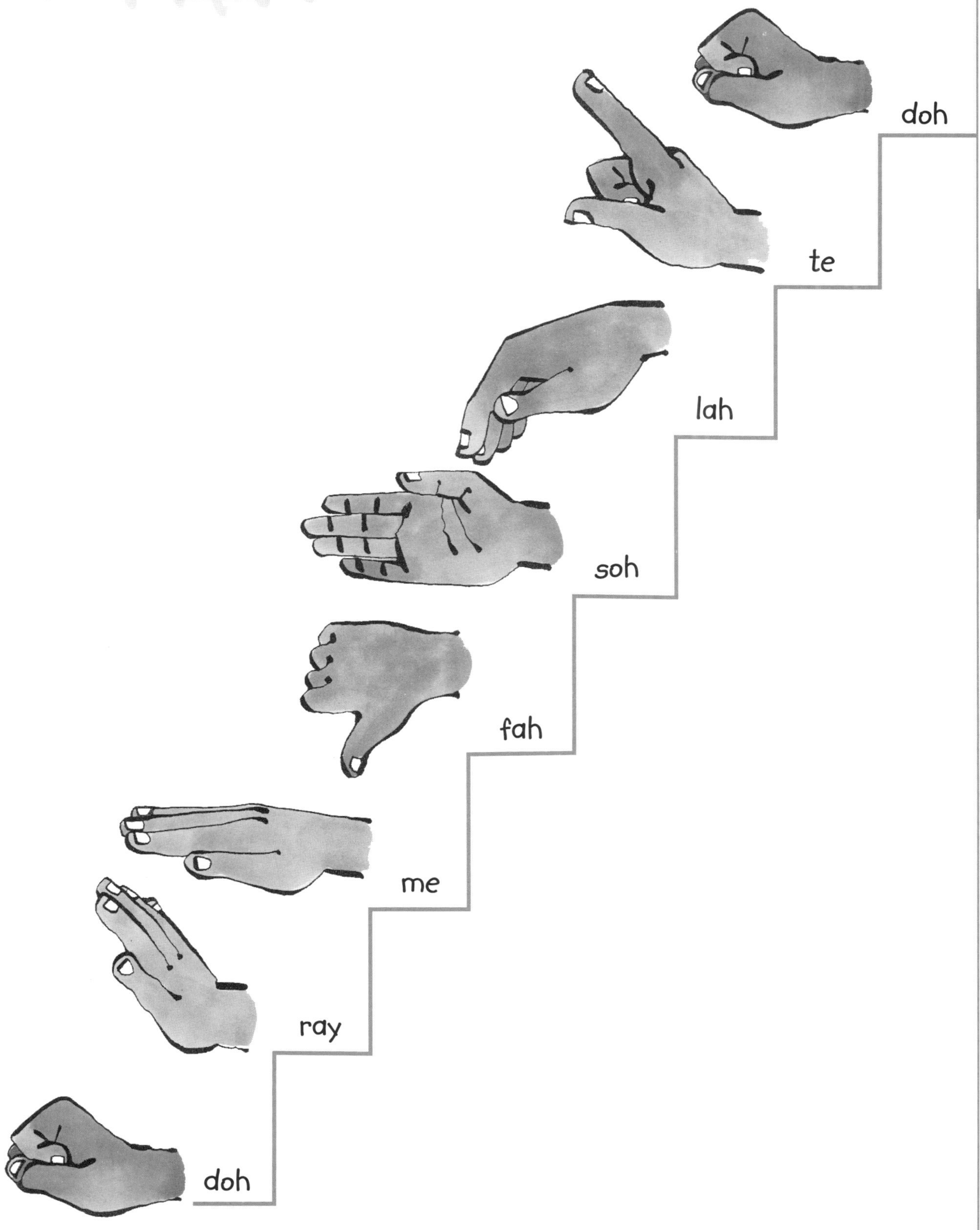

Prompt sheet

Tonic Sol-fa names and hand signs

Do-re-mi second melody

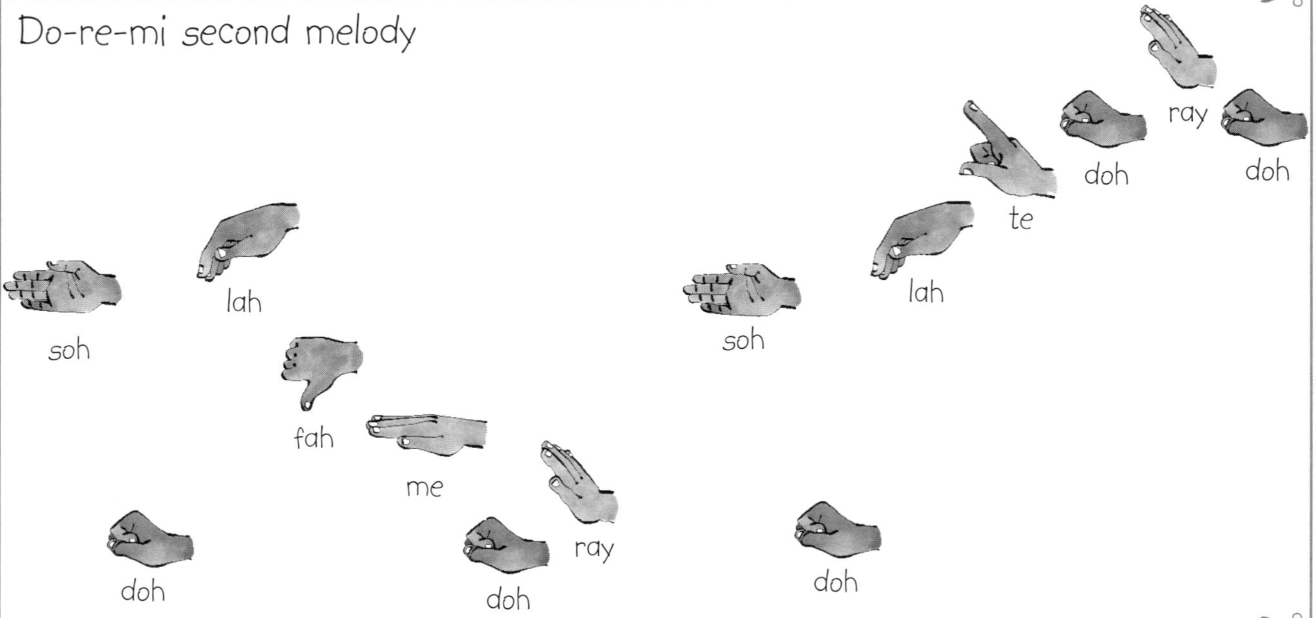

Melodic ostinato

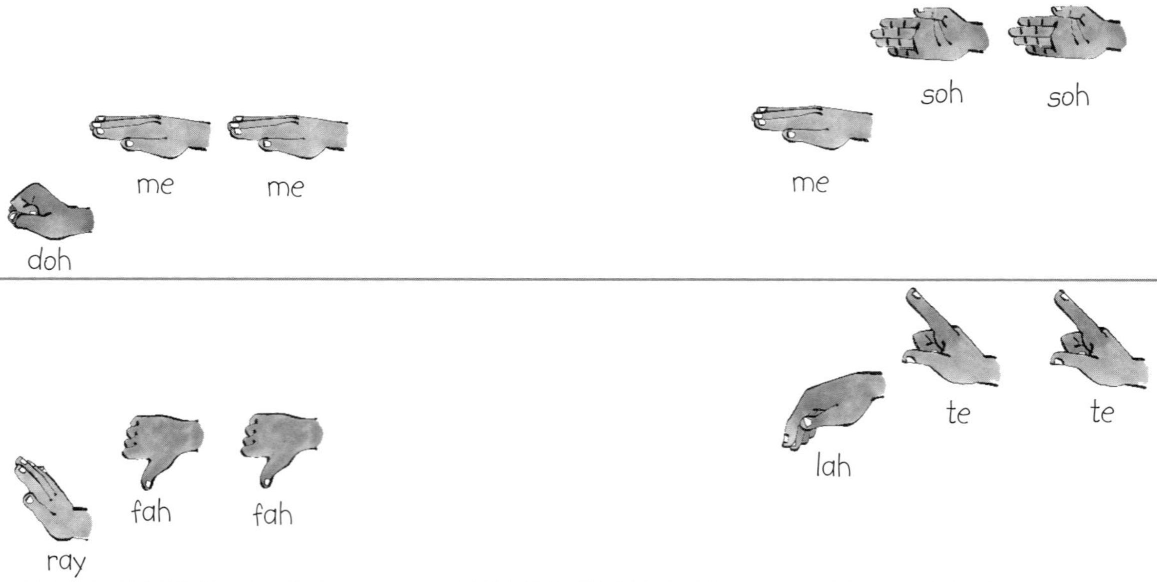

DO-RE-MI

1 Discuss the structure of the complete *Do-re-mi* song

p32 50

- Listen to a performance of the complete song, ***Do-re-mi*** *(track 50)*. Ask the children to describe the structure:
  - first melody;
  - second melody;
  - second melody with new words and a melodic ostinato accompaniment;
  - first melody + ending.
- All join in singing with the CD, using the Kodaly hand signs to help feel the pitch movement *(use the* ***Prompt sheet*** *photocopiable, if necessary).*

2 Learn to perform a melodic ostinato accompaniment with the second melody in *Do-re-mi*

p32 50-51

- Listen to the melodic ostinato accompaniment *(track 51).*
- Practise singing the melodic ostinato very slowly without the CD, using the hand signs on the ***Prompt sheet*** photocopiable to help the children feel the pitch movement.
- When the melody is secure, sing it at the faster tempo on the CD.
- All sing ***Do-re-mi*** with track 50. The class divides in half for the middle section of the song: one half sings the second melody and the other half the melodic ostinato.
(If your CD player can fast forward within the track, practise this section separately before singing the song as a whole.)

Teaching tips

- You might like to appoint leaders to help direct the singing.
- Some children may like to follow the hand signs on the *Prompt sheet* photocopiable as they sing.

3 Perform the complete *Do-re-mi* song

p32 50 52

- Rehearse the complete song in the structure given on track 50. First practise singing with track 50, and when everyone is confident, perform the song with the backing track only *(track 52).*
- Perform the song to a friendly audience.

JIBBER JABBER

1 Sing the song *Jibber jabber* (53)

- Teach the first voice part of *Jibber jabber* using track 53.

Vs Jibber jabber, gabble, babble, cackle, clack and prate,
Twiddle, twaddle, mutter, stutter, utter, splutter, blate,
Chatter, patter, tattle, prattle, chew the rag and crack,
Spiel and spout and spit it out, tell the world and quack.

Ch Jibber, jibber jabber,
Jibber jabber, jibber jabber, you hoo hoo hoo.
Jibber, jibber jabber,
Jibber jabber, jibber jabber, YOU!

- As a class, think about where the phrases are in the song.
(Each line of the song is a phrase and a suitable place to breathe.)
- Sing the song again, all tracing an arc in the air for each phrase.

2 Learn a second voice part and xylophone accompaniment to *Jibber jabber* (p35) (53-55)

- Listen to the second voice part *(track 54)*, all following the hand signs on the ***Jibbery extras*** photocopiable.
- Teach the melody with the hand signs to help the children learn the pitch shape of the melody. Practise slowly without the CD all making the hand signs for each syllable.

Doh me soh fah me ray doh,
Te ray fah me ray doh ray,
Doh me soh fah me ray doh,
Ray soh doh.

When the notes are secure, practise singing at the faster tempo given on track 54.

- Listen to track 55. Ask the children to describe the xylophone melody which accompanies the chorus.
(It moves up then down by step like a scale.)
- Invite as many children as possible to take turns to play the xylophone accompaniment on tuned percussion using the photocopiable to learn the notes. Practise playing the accompaniment with track 53.

Teaching tips

- Listen again to the sample performance on track 53 to revise the structure of the piece.
- If necessary, the children could have copies of the *Jibbery extras* photocopiable to follow when performing the second melody in the verse and the xylophone accompaniment in the chorus.

3 Appraise a performance of *Jibber jabber* (37) (53)

- Rehearse *Jibber jabber* with track 53. You will need a group to sing the second voice part and a group to play the xylophone accompaniment in the chorus, and everyone else to sing the song.
- When everyone is confident performing with track 53, rehearse the song with the backing track *(track 37)*.
- Record a performance of the song, then listen back to discuss:
  - whether all the singers' words were clear;
  - whether the second part and xylophone accompaniment were performed in time with the singers;
  - whether the performance was lively and expressive.

Jibbery extras

Second voice part – verse

1 2 3 4 1 2 3 4

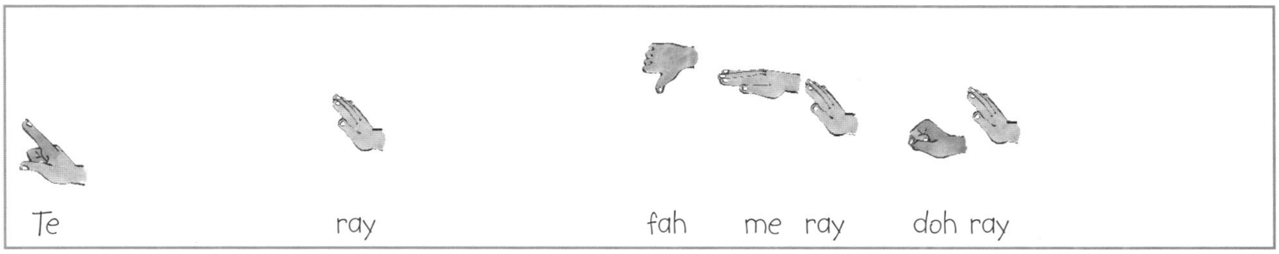

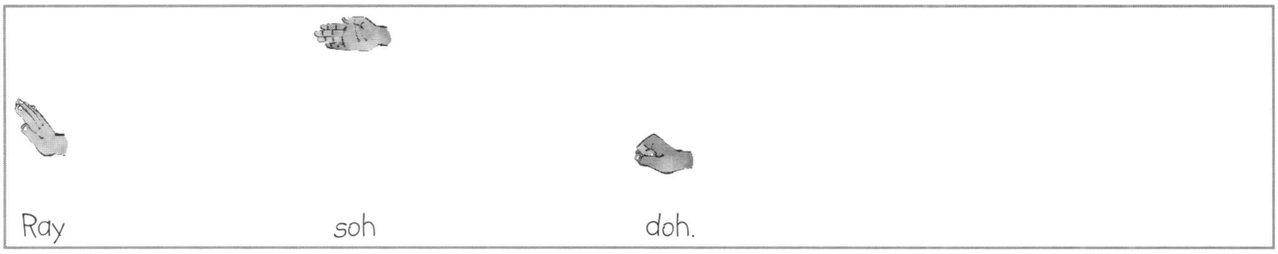

Xylophone accompaniment – chorus

1 2 3 4 1 2 3 4 1 2 3 4 1 2 3 4

(repeat)

PROGRAMME MUSIC

1 Listen to two contrasting pieces of programme music

56-57

- Explain that music which paints a picture, creates a mood or tells a story is called 'Programme music'.
- Listen to an extract of ***Euphoria*** *(track 56)* without telling the children the title. Ask what the music makes the children feel or imagine.
- Ask what instruments the children can hear in the music. *(Steel pans are the most prominent instruments.)*
- Listen to ***Spooky Spinney*** *(track 57)*. Ask the children to describe what they imagine listening to the music.

Teaching tips

- You may need to listen to the extracts of music several times.
- Each time a child suggests an idea, ask them why they think that.
- It does not matter if the children have different ideas to those mentioned here.

Background information

- Steel pans are traditional in Caribbean music. They are made from recycled oil drums. One end of the drum is beaten into a concave surface from which ellipse-shaped portions are raised to make the different notes. Steel pans are played with rubber-ended wooden or metal sticks.

2 Discuss how music creates mental images

56-57

- Discuss how the composers of ***Euphoria*** and ***Spooky Spinney*** create the mood or image:
  - ***Euphoria*** *(track 56)*
    The beat of the music makes us feel like dancing; the high note at the start of each phrase gives it a very happy sound; the melody is very simple and catchy which again makes the music dance-like ...
  - ***Spooky Spinney*** *(track 57)*
    The music has a vocal part that sets the scene - walking late through Spooky Spinney. The narrator sounds frightened and gets gradually louder to build the sense that something is about to happen. Low notes give a sense of suspense; they move by step which reminds us that the person is walking slowly and something spooky may be following. There is also a howling, spooky wind sound effect.

3 Play *Tambourine talk* to express moods using instruments and vocal sounds

- Give each child a tambourine or other untuned percussion instrument and divide the class into pairs. *(Pass instruments round as you play the game if there are not enough).*
- Play *Tambourine talk*:
  - begin by suggesting some words which might describe a conversation, eg 'happy', 'secretive', 'angry', 'lively', or 'noisy';
  - each pair chooses a word, and using the instruments only, performs a 'conversation' in the style of that word while everyone else listens *(eg for 'angry' they might play their instruments in loud, fast bursts as if shouting at one another);*
  - the rest of the class guess the mood of the conversation.

  (Encourage the children to think about: the speed of the conversation - tempo; how loudly they converse - dynamics; the quality of the sound they produce - timbre; how long each sound lasts - duration ...)
- Discuss how different moods were created. Ask whether it was difficult on some instruments to create suitable timbres for particular moods *(eg to 'talk' secretively using a cowbell).*
- Repeat the game, but this time the children converse with each other using vocal sounds, but no real words!

DAY OFF

1 Listen to the song *Day off* 58-59

- Listen to ***Day off*** *(track 58)* and ask the children what the song is about. *(Someone imagining what it would be like to travel around the world.)*
- Ask where the person went in their imagination and what they did. *(Watched the sunrise on the Great Wall of China, played with porpoises in the Caspian Sea, drank tea in Darjeeling ...)*
- Listen to the accompaniment for ***Day off*** *(track 59)*, and all pick up the beat of the music, tapping fingertips on knees. Invite volunteers to jog on the spot in time with the beat.

Teaching tip

- You may need to listen to the song several times to hear the many different places visited.

2 Compose jogging music for a *Running round the world* class composition 60

- Ask the class to imagine they are marathon runners jogging round the world. Listen to track 60. Explain that this is one way music might represent someone jogging.
- Invite volunteers to suggest other ways that jogging might be represented using tuned or untuned percussion instruments.
- As a class, use some of the ideas suggested to create jogging music which the whole class can perform in time with a steady beat.
- Rehearse the class jogging music.

3 Plan the *Running round the world* class composition

p38

- Look at the pictures on the ***Around the world*** photocopiable. Explain that these are six scenes visited in the song ***Day off***.
- Divide the class into six groups, one for each of the scenes on the photocopiable.

  Explain that each group will compose a descriptive piece of music inspired by the mood of their scene. Each group will perform their composition in turn, linked by the jogging music created in activity 2 which represents travelling from place to place.
- Each group researches their scene and gains an understanding of where it is, what the mood would be like and any other factual information that may be represented musically *(eg the porpoise group might research the way porpoises move, the Nepal group might research the climate in Nepal and how high the mountains are ...)*.
- Each group makes notes of their work for the next lesson.

Teaching tip

- Groups may decide to research and plan their composition on one of the other places visited in the song *Day off*.

Around the world

Great Wall of China

Porpoises in the Caspian Sea

Climbing mountains in Nepal

Dance band in Mexico

Sahara desert

Limbo dancing on a tropical island

IN THE MOOD

1 Discuss the mood behind each scene of the *Running round the world* composition

- Ask each group to imagine how they would feel in the scene they chose last lesson *(eg exhausted climbing mountains in Nepal; exhilarated with a sense of freedom watching the sunrise over the Great Wall of China; happy and energetic dancing to the music of the mariachi dance band in Mexico ...)*
- Encourage the children to think about how to express these feelings in music *(eg when exhausted, play slowly; when exhilarated, play gently; when happy and energetic, compose a dance-like melody ...)*
- Each group then discusses the instruments they would like to use for the scene they are creating.
(Encourage the children to hear the sound in their heads, identify which instrument they are hearing and how it might be played, and then try the instrument to check if it sounds as they want.)

Teaching tips

- It is important for the children's musical development to practise internalising sounds - imagining the sound an instrument will make before trying it out.
- Encourage the children to think about the different elements of music in their compositions:

tempo - eg when exhausted climbing mountains, play slowly;

dynamics - eg if feeling calm and relaxed, play quietly;

rhythm - eg when happy, play lively dance rhythms;

duration - eg if tired, play long sustained notes;

pitch - eg when a porpoise jumps out of the water, leap from a low note to a higher one;

texture - if lonely, use fewer instruments;

timbre - explore using different instruments to create specific effects.

2 Compose the scenes for the *Running round the world* class composition

- Each group develops the musical ideas for their composition about a chosen scene and starts putting the ideas together.
(Suggest that each group's composition should last no more than 30 seconds.)
- As well as communicating the mood of the scene they are visiting, encourage each group to represent some of the physical aspects of their scene using their research in lesson 2 *(eg a limbo dancer would limbo gradually lower and lower - this could be represented by playing descending notes on a xylophone).*
- Encourage each group to think about how to structure their composition.
(They might like to appoint a leader to direct their group.)

3 Share the work in progress

- Each group presents their work to the class.
- After each group's performance, encourage the class to say what mood they felt was being represented. If this is different to what was intended, the group might wish to make some changes *(but remember that a composer's work is always open to interpretation).*

RUNNING ROUND THE WORLD

1 Decide upon an order for the *Running round the world* composition

p38 p41

- As a class, decide a suitable order for the scenes in the class composition. Follow this overall structure:
  - jogging music
  - scene 1
  - jogging music
  - scene 2
  - jogging music
  - scene 3 etc

  Ask the children to devise a logic for the order of the scenes *(eg follow a route around a globe, or decide the order based on the musical effect).*
- Create a class score for the composition by cutting out each scene from the ***Around the world*** photocopiable *(p38)* and placing it in order on the ***Globe trotting*** photocopiable *(p41).*

Teaching tips

- Try to create a balanced overall effect for the composition, eg:
  - place musically contrasting pieces one after the other;
  - avoid playing two similar pieces one after the other.
- Try out different orders to see which the children prefer.

2 Rehearse each scene of the *Running round the world* class composition

- In the same groups as last lesson, the children rehearse their scenes.
- When everyone is ready, the whole class rehearses the jogging music from the second lesson.
- Decide as a class how each scene will link into and out of the jogging music *(eg the jogging music could fade out before each scene begins and then fade in again afterwards).*

3 Perform and record the *Running round the world* class composition

- Perform the whole piece and record it.
- Listen to the recording and discuss:
  - how effective each scene is in creating a mood;
  - how expressive each mood is *(eg use of loud/quiet, fast/slow ...)*;
  - how effective the jogging music is as a link between scenes;
  - what the children would change about their performance, if anything.

Globe trotting

SEASHORE

1 Discuss the images in the poem, *Seashore*

61 pic 1-6

- Listen to the poem, and ask the children what it is about. *(The seashore.)*

Pretty shells washed onto the sand,
Sand a golden yellow colour,
Colour in the blue of the sea,
Sea with gentle lapping waves,
Waves clouded with green seaweed,
Seaweed clinging to the breakwaters.
Breakwaters stand ugly in the water,
Water envelops the cliffs,
Cliffs with bare white faces.
Faces of donkeys and faces of people,
People lying tanned in deckchairs,
Deckchairs lying disregarded.
Disregarded boats tied to the piers,
Piers standing rooted in pebbles,
Pebbles worn smooth by the water,
Water collecting in the rock pools.
Rock pools inhabited by limpets,
Limpets stuck to surrounding rocks,
Rocks distorted like bits of wood,
Wood washed up along the shore,
Shore with litter, synthetic rope.

- Ask what the children notice about the last word of each line and the first word of the next. *(They are the same.)*
- Ask what the effect of this is. *(Those words are stressed and create a stronger image in the mind.)*
- Listen again and identify the positive images in the poem *(eg pretty shells, pebbles worn smooth by the water ...)* and negative images *(eg deckchairs lying disregarded, the shore covered in litter ...).*
- Show the children pictures of some of the images from the poem on the CD-ROM and check that everyone understands the vocabulary in the poem.

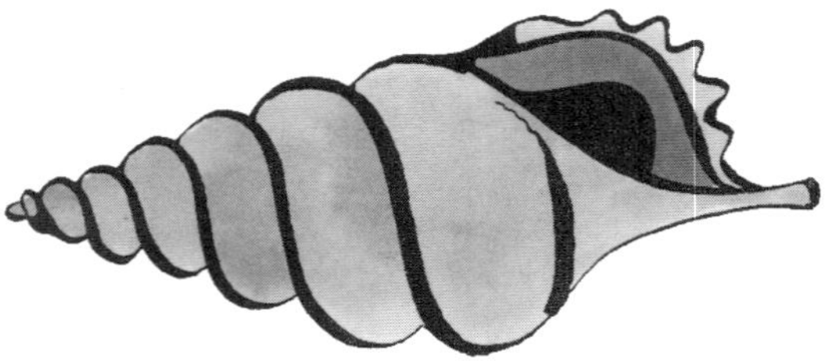

2 Plan group compositions based on *Seashore*

- Divide the class into groups to plan a piece of programme music based on the poem, *Seashore.*
- Explain that each group's composition must:
  – represent two contrasting images from the poem;
  – include a melodic or rhythmic ostinato for all or part of the composition.
- All listen to the poem again, then each group discusses which positive and which negative image they will represent in their composition and how they will include the ostinato.

3 Begin the seashore compositions

- Each group thinks about which instruments they will use in their composition and how they might be played for best effect.
- Each group starts trying out their ideas and putting their piece together. Encourage the children to consider the structure of their composition *(eg will the music represent the two images from the poem one after the other, or alternate between the two contrasting moods as if in a conversation).*
- Encourage each group to make a note of their ideas for next lesson.

Teaching tips

- Children who have not done a lot of group work may find it difficult to work like this and may need support in their decision-making routines, sharing instruments and listening to each other's ideas.
- Check that everyone remembers that an ostinato is a repeated pattern.
- Encourage the children to explore electronic keyboards and their voices for appropriate sound effects. They might also use everyday sounds, such as running water.
- Give the children access to the pictures on the CD-ROM for inspiration while they work.

MOODY SEAS

1 Develop the seashore compositions

pic 1-6

- Each group develops their seashore composition. Remind the children of the tasks they have to complete in their composition *(see p42)*, and have the CD-ROM available to show the pictures of the seashore.
- Give each group time and space in which to rehearse their performance. Encourage each group to be as expressive as possible. *(They might like to appoint a leader to direct their group.)*

Teaching tip

- Visit each group as they rehearse to offer support and guidance.

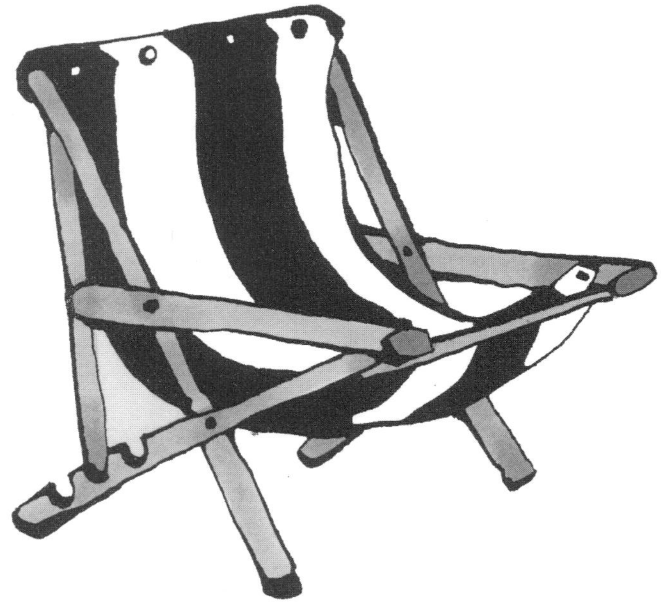

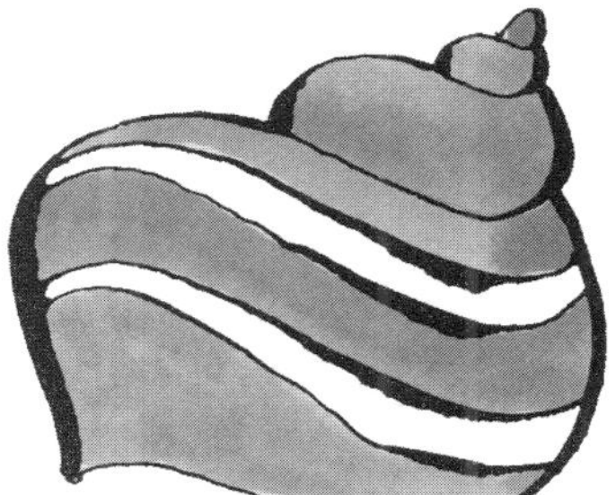

2 Perform and record each group's seashore composition

- Record each group performing their seashore composition to the rest of the class.

3 Listen to the recordings and evaluate the seashore compositions

- Listen to each group's recording in turn, and invite the group to explain how the piece is structured. Invite other members of the class to ask questions.
- As a class, help each group to evaluate their composition. Have a mental check-list of things to think about for each piece, eg
  - did the composition succeed in representing the images from the poem?
  - was the contrast between the images well represented?
  - did the group complete the two tasks?
  - how effective was the ostinato?
  - did the composition appear to be well-constructed?
  - did the group appear to have considered carefully which instruments and sound effects to use?
  - did the performance include expression - loud and quiet; fast and slow?
  - did the performance appear to be well-organised?
  - did all members of the group contribute to the preparation and performance of the composition?

CROWDED CITY

1 Listen to *Crowded city* and identify sound signals

62

- Listen to ***Crowded city*** *(track 62)*. Ask the children what sounds of a busy main road they can hear represented in the music *(eg car horn, pelican crossing and a bicycle bell ...)*.
- Explain that the sounds they have identified are all signals, and ask the children to explain what a signal is. *(A signal is an action, sound, gesture, or sign used as a means of communication.)*
- Listen to track 62 again and make a list of all the signals the children can hear.
- Ask the children to think of any other sound signals used in their community, eg fire alarm, fog horn, ambulance ... Ask what the signals mean.

Teaching tips

- To work something out by ear, listen carefully to the intervals between the notes:
  - is the next note higher, lower or the same?
  - is there a big leap or do the notes move by step?
- Encourage the children to sing the melodies quietly to help them work out the pitch.
- Listen to the CD several times as you work out the pitch.

2 Explore some musical features of sound signals

p45 63

- Listen to some melodic sound signals *(track 63)*.
- As a class, work out the melody of each signal using chime bars, and write the answer on the ***Melodic signals*** photocopiable. *(The starting notes have been given.)*

Answers:

1. Door bell: G E
2. Public announcement: C G E
3. Passenger announcement: C E G
4. Westminster chimes: B G A D D A B G
5. Church bells: C C' B A G F E D C

3 Discuss the sound signals in *Crowded city* and other signals used in the community

62

- Listen again to track 62. Ask the children what makes these signals sound different from those in track 63. *(The composer does not use the real life sounds of the signals, he represents the signals in the music using musical instruments.)*
- Discuss other signals used in the community that are not sound signals *(eg traffic lights, zebra crossing, car indicators, arm signals when riding a bike ...)*.

Melodic signals

Door bell

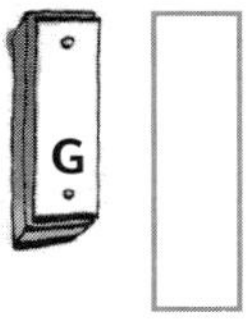

Public announcement

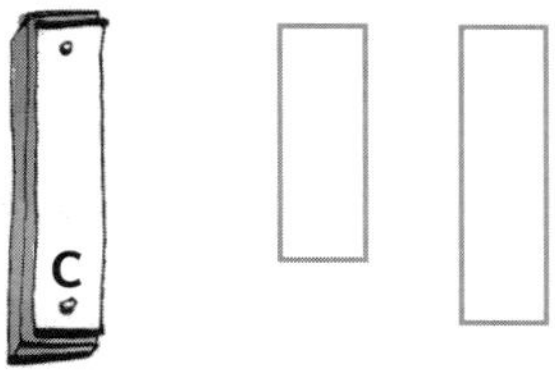

Passenger announcement

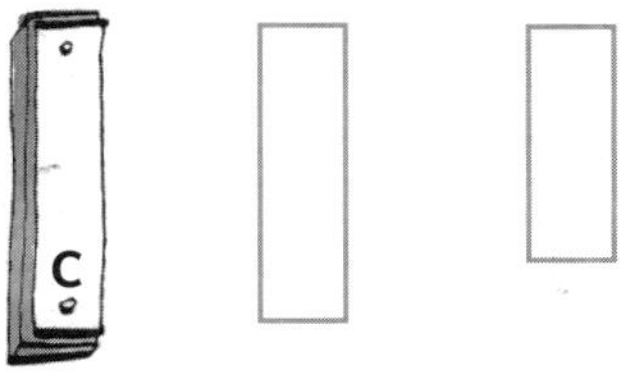

Westminster chimes

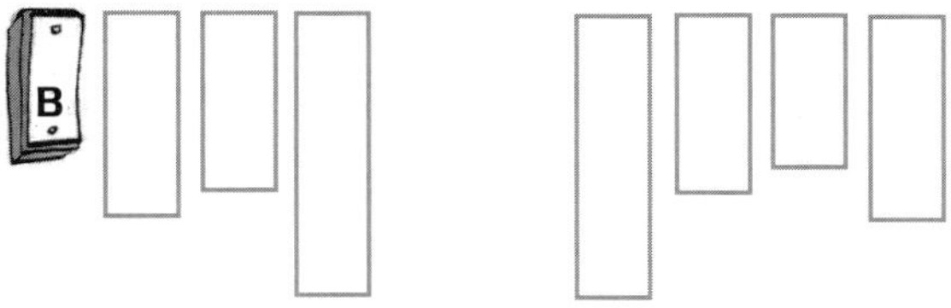

Wedding bells

FOLLOW THE LEADER

1 Identify how a musical signal is used to control volume (64)

- Listen to an extract of *Baris gede 'bandrangan' (track 64).*
- Explain that the drummer leads the performance. Listen again and ask what happens to the music when the drummer plays loudly.
(Everyone else plays loudly.)
- Listen a third time and ask what happens when the drummer plays quietly.
(Everyone else plays quietly.)

Background information

- *Baris gede 'bandrangan'* is a modern piece of gamelan music from Bali, composed by I Wayan Beratha.
- *Gamelan* is the name of a group of instruments (mainly tuned percussion) as well as the music itself. Most gamelan have about twenty players, but some are much larger.
- A *baris gede* is a ritual spear dance for men; this one is called 'bandrangan' after the tassel attached to the spear's handle.

2 Practise combining different rhythm patterns (65-67)

- Listen to five rhythm patterns *(track 65)*. Each pattern lasts three beats and is performed twice on the CD. All copy each rhythm pattern using body percussion in the gaps.
(Repeat the track until everyone is confident copying each rhythm.)
- Invite individuals to invent new rhythm patterns for the class to copy using body percussion. Each pattern should last only three beats and be repeated. Some children may like to consider inventing harder patterns. Copy the three rhythm patterns on track 66.
- Divide the class into small groups of four or five. Everyone in the group chooses one of the rhythm patterns they have rehearsed, or invents their own pattern using body percussion. Each group practises playing their patterns at the same time to the same steady beat.
(You might like to listen to the CD tracks again.)
- Each group rehearses combining their patterns in time to a backing track *(track 67)*.

Teaching tips

- Some children may need to find a way to write down their rhythm pattern to help them remember.
- Check that the leader gives a good clear signal that everyone can see, and that everyone works hard to keep together.
- Help the children keep the patterns together by playing the beat throughout.

3 Perform rhythm patterns following a class leader (67)

- As a class, practise combining all the individual rhythm patterns from activity 2 with the backing track *(track 67)*.
- Then, without the backing track, invite a volunteer to be the leader. The leader will signal to the rest of the class to change volume, by playing the following rhythm on a cowbell at the new volume:

1   2 + 3

The class perform their patterns in time to a steady beat, and follow the leader's volume signals.
- Let as many children as possible be the leader.

cowbell

INSPECTOR MORSE

1 Play the *All change signal game* 65-67

- Sitting in a circle, all choose a three-beat rhythmic ostinato to perform on body percussion. Practise combining all the rhythm patterns in time with the backing track *(track 67)*.
  (The children may use one of the rhythm patterns from last lesson, or invent a new pattern. Listen to tracks 65-66 for examples.)
- Give some children an untuned percussion instrument *(one between four is a good guide)*. Repeat the activity. As they play this time, everyone pays particular attention to the pattern that the person either side of them is playing.
  (Check that the children have heard their neighbours' patterns by stopping the CD and asking a child to demonstrate them. Were they correct?)
- Invite a volunteer to be the leader. The game uses two different signals:
  – three loud steady beats on a cowbell in time with the CD signals everyone to change to the pattern of the person sitting on their left;
  – three quiet steady beats on a cowbell in time with the CD signals everyone to change to the pattern of the person sitting on their right.
- Once they have settled into their new pattern they should notice the new patterns to their left and right.

Teaching tips

- Listen to make sure everyone plays in time with the steady beat.
- Each time the game is repeated, everyone passes their instrument to the person on their left.
- Encourage the leader to leave a long gap between signals to allow the new patterns to be established, and for each individual to notice the new patterns to their left and right.

Background information

- Morse code was developed in the early 1800s.
- Morse code consists of combinations of long and short signals known as dits and dahs.
- The idea belonged to Samuel Morse who designed a pattern for every letter of the alphabet. Each letter is a long or a short or a combination of the two. He could then use an electronic pulse of long or short sounds, or a light beam to communicate.
- *Inspector Morse* was composed by Barrington Pheloung in 1991 for the title music of the television crime series called *Inspector Morse*.

2 Listen to the use of Morse code in *Inspector Morse* 68-69

- Listen to track 68 and ask the children what they hear.
  (An electronic beep and violin playing long and short notes. The notes make a pattern that is played twice.)
- Write the following pattern on the board for everyone to follow as you listen again:

  — —   — — —   ● — ●   ● ● ●   ●

- Explain that the electronic beeps are Morse code and are used to communicate the letters of the alphabet. Tell the children that this extract of music is from a piece called ***Inspector Morse.*** The pattern spells:

— —	— — —	● — ●	● ● ●	●
M	O	R	S	E

- Listen to an extract of ***Inspector Morse*** *(track 69)* and ask the children if they hear the opening pattern again.
  (Yes, it is played throughout the piece.)
- Ask whether the pattern is always heard as the electronic beeps.
  (No, the pattern is played on instruments as well.)

3 Explore the Morse code alphabet p48 70-71

- Use the ***Morse code*** photocopiable to show the class the Morse code alphabet.
- All listen to track 70 and copy the letters of the alphabet.
- Listen to track 71. In pairs, work out what the letters are, and fill in the blanks at the bottom of the photocopiable. *Answer:*

● ● ●	● ●	— — ●	— ●	● —	● — ● ●
S	I	G	N	A	L

- When everyone has worked out the word, all join in tapping the Morse code with fingertips on knees.

Morse code

a	• —	n	— •
b	— • • •	o	— — —
c	— • — •	p	• — — •
d	— • •	q	— — • —
e	•	r	• — •
f	• • — •	s	• • •
g	— — •	t	—
h	• • • •	u	• • —
i	• •	v	• • • —
j	• — — —	w	• — —
k	— • —	x	— • • —
l	• — • •	y	— • — —
m	— —	z	— — • •

Track 71 - What's the word?

Write the Morse code letters in the boxes and then decode them.

The first letter is done for you.

• • •					
s	___	___	___	___	___

THE SIGNAL SONG

1 Listen to the use of Morse code in the melody of *The signal song*

p50 72

- Listen to ***The signal song*** *(track 72).*
- Listen again, and all pay particular attention to the rhythm. It is made up of the letters of the word 'signal' in Morse code. The letters S I G N make up the call and the A and the L repeated form the response.
- All follow the 'Signal' rhythm on the ***Signal call/Signal response*** photocopiable while listening to track 72. Join in with the rhythm of the call and the response by all tapping fingertips on knees.

s • • •
i • •
g — — •
n — •
a • —
l • — • •

Teaching tip

- Instruments such as recorders, violins or electronic keyboards are better than tuned percussion for making sustained sounds. Encourage any children who play these instruments to bring them to the lesson.

2 Sing the melodies of *The signal song* call and response to Morse code syllables

p50 73

- Listen to ***The signal song*** sung in track 73, and follow it on the ***Signal call/Signal response*** photocopiable.
- All join in singing the call and the response as dits and dahs with track 73. Practise this several times.
- Divide the class in half. One half sings the call and the other half the response, then swap over.

3 Learn to play the melody of the call in *The signal song*

p50 72-73

- Invite volunteers to learn to play the melody of the call in ***The signal song*** on instruments using the ***Signal call/Signal response*** photocopiable and track 73. *(Encourage the volunteers to listen carefully to the CD to make sure of the rhythm.)*
- Invite the instrumentalists to play the call with track 72 whilst the rest of the class sing the call and the response as dits and dahs. *(Let as many children as possible have a go at playing an instrument.)*

Call:

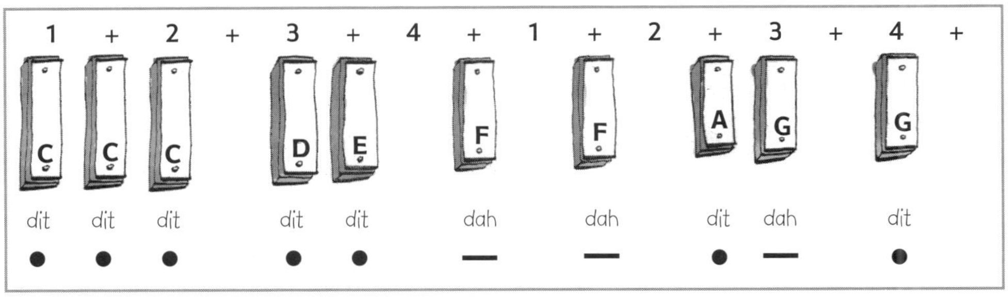

Signal call

1	+	2	+	3	+	4	+	1	+	2	+	3	+	4	+
C	C	C		D	E		F		F		A	G		G	
dit	dit	dit		dit	dit		dah		dah		dit	dah		dit	
●	●	●		●	●		—		—		●	—		●	

Signal response

1	+	2	+	3	+	4	+	1	+	2	+	3	+	4	+
C	C		C	C		C	C	C	C		C	C		C	C
dit	dah		dit	dah		dit	dit	dit	dah		dit	dah		dit	dit
●	—		●	—		●	●	●	—		●	—		●	●

IS IT A SIGNAL?

1 Revise the melody of *The signal song*

p50 72-73

- Revise the previous activity *(lesson 4, activity 3)*. Instrumentalists perform the melody of the call, and singers perform the melody of the whole song to track 72, using the ***Signal call/Signal response*** photocopiable as a guide.
  (The singers might like to practise with track 73 before singing with the backing track alone.)
- Repeat the activity, with a third group joining in to play the melody of the response on recorders or electronic keyboards.

2 Discuss the word setting of *The signal song*

p52 74

- Listen to ***The signal song*** with a verse of sample lyrics *(track 74)*.

1	+	2	+	3	+	4	+	1	+	2	+	3	+	4	+	1
C	C	C		D	E		F		F		A	G		G		G
Is	it	a		sig	- nal?		Who		called		the	fire		bri	-	gade?
Sod	- den	black		ash	- es,		all		of		the	lives		were		saved.

(Explain that the lyrics have been written to fit the rhythm of the call, but with an extra note at the end to finish the phrase.)

- Practise singing the words with track 74.
- Divide the class into five groups. Explain that each group is going to work together to create their own lyrics for a verse *(two lines)* of ***The signal song***.
- Discuss the different types of signals there are in society. Use the ***Ideas sheet*** photocopiable for inspiration. Consider:
  - sound signals such as a telephone ring, school bell, fire alarm;
  - visual universal signals such as red cross or red crescent, white flag for surrender;
  - contact signals such as shaking hands and other greetings.
- Discuss why signals are important in our world.

3 Invent words for *The signal song*

p50

- Each group discusses which signal to write about. Each verse should start with the words: 'Is it a signal?', eg

  Is it a signal? Where can we find first aid?
  Bandages, water, easing the pain we've made.
  or
  Is it a signal? When can we go for lunch?
  When you stop talking, then there'll be time to munch!
- Each group invents lyrics for a verse of ***The signal song***.
  (Make sure each group's lyrics fit the rhythm of the call as explained in activity 2. They do not write lyrics for the rhythm of the response.)
- Invite each group to recite the lyrics of their verse to the class. Encourage the class to offer suggestions for improvement.

Teaching tips

- Each group needs at least one member who feels confident about playing or singing the melody.
- Each group may like to have access to a tuned percussion instrument or electronic keyboard and the *Signal call/Signal response* photocopiable to rehearse their lyrics as they go along.

Ideas sheet

Fire engine

Police car

School bell

Door bell

Namaste

Hand shake

SIGNAL TO PERFORM

1 Rehearse the ideas for *The signal song* 72

- The same groups as last week rehearse singing their invented verses with the backing track *(track 72)*. The rest of the class helps each group to keep in time by tapping the rhythm of the melody using two fingers on their palm while they sing.
- Encourage each group to choose one person to play the melody of the call on tuned percussion, an instrument from home or electronic keyboard, as the rest of the group sing.
  (Another instrumentalist might perform the response.)
- Each group practises playing and singing along with the backing track.

2 Add appropriate signal sounds and/or actions to *The signal song* 74

- Listen again to ***The signal song*** sung with sample lyrics *(track 74)*. Listen for the fire engine sound effect after the first line.
- Encourage those groups which chose a sound signal to include a sound effect after the first line. Those groups which chose a visual or contact signal might perform an action at the same point in the song.
- Each group rehearses singing, playing the melody and including a sound effect or action.

3 Rehearse then record the class performance of *The signal song* 72

- Decide an order for the groups to perform in, and write each group's verse on the board so everyone may join in.
- Rehearse the groups performing their verses in time to the backing track one after the other.
- Think of a way to finish the piece, for example the class might write a final verse, eg:

  These are our signals, this is the song we've made.
  Working together, making our music to say, SIGNALS!

- When everyone is ready, record the class song.
- Listen back and invite individuals to suggest the three best things about the performance.

Teaching tips

- After listening to the recording, the children might decide on aspects of their performance they would like to improve.
- If so, allow each group a few minutes to prepare and then record a second performance.
- Ask the children whether their second performance was an improvement.

ASSORTED ANIMALS

1 Discuss the composer's description of a firebird in *Dance of the firebird*

75

- Listen to *Dance of the firebird* and ask the children to imagine what the firebird looks like *(eg is it large, small, colourful, light, heavy, graceful, awkward ...?).*

  Ask them to give their reasons *(eg children may suggest it is quite large because there are several instruments playing, or small because the instruments playing the melody are quite high-pitched).*

- Listen to the track again and ask what instruments the children can hear.
  (This piece of music is performed by a full orchestra. The high melodic instruments that the children may hear are flutes and clarinets. They are accompanied by string instruments - violins, violas, cellos and double basses - and harp. They may also identify trumpets and French horns playing loud pecking sounds in the middle of the track.)

- Listen to the track a third time and ask the children to imagine how the firebird is moving.
  (For example the children might suggest that the high repeated notes represent the bird pecking, or that the sudden upward rushing movements in the melody are like a bird spreading its wings and taking off ...)

Background information

- *The firebird* is a ballet by the Russian composer Stravinsky (1882–1971). The ballet was first performed in Paris in 1910. It tells the legend of the firebird who helps the young prince Ivan Tsarevich kill the green-taloned ogre Kashchei, and free his captives.
- The gnu is a large grazing antelope, native to Southern and East Africa. It is also known as wildebeest. It has a long shaggy head, hooked horns and a long tail.

2 Discuss the use of words and music in *The bellipong*

76

- Listen to ***The bellipong***. Ask the children which words are used to describe the bellipong.
  (The bellipong is described as fat, round and slow with a low, wobbly tummy.)

- Listen to the track again, and ask how the music assists the words in describing the animal.
  (The music is slow, is sung at a very low pitch, and is accompanied by low-pitched instruments.)

- Ask the children how the music is different from ***Dance of the firebird***.
  *(**The bellipong** is a song accompanied by a much simpler, thinner texture. It uses mainly low notes. **Dance of the firebird** uses many instruments, providing a much thicker texture. It uses mainly high notes for the melody.)*

3 Learn *A gnu* and consider how the words and music describe the animal's personality

77

- Listen to ***A gnu*** then ask the children to describe the gnu's personality *(eg the children might think that the gaps after the words imply that it is an unhurried and very polite animal; they might think that the melody sounds slightly cheeky; from the words, they might consider the gnu to be rather vain in the way it considers itself superior to other animals).*

- Learn to sing the first verse of the song.

I'm a g-nu, I'm a g-nu,
The g-nicest work of g-nature in the zoo!
I'm a g-nu, how do you do?
You really ought to k-now w-ho's w-ho.
I'm a g-nu, spelt G.N.U.
I'm g-not a camel or a kangaroo,
So let me introduce,
I'm g-neither man or moose,
Oh, g-no, g-no, g-no,
I'm a g-nu!

Teaching tip

- These ideas are suggestions only, the children will have their own imaginative ideas about the gnu's personality.

A GNU

1 Sing *A gnu* using voices expressively

77-79

- Revise the first verse of *A gnu* using track 77.
- All listen to track 78 and discuss how it is different from track 77. *(It is sung lower in pitch, more slowly, and with a very creaky voice.)*
- Explain that this is how the song might be sung by a very old gnu. All join in singing as old gnus with track 78. Ask the children to describe how they changed their voices.
  (They sang more slowly to indicate an older creature moving more slowly. They made their voices creaky and shaky.)
- All listen to track 79. Ask the children to suggest which group of gnus might be singing this time, indicating their reasons.
  (Young gnus - the melody is higher in pitch which implies a younger animal; it is performed faster which also indicates a young, more agile animal.)
- Listen again to track 79 and ask the children to describe how the voice has been changed to represent a young gnu.
  (The voice has been changed electronically to make it squeaky and high pitched as young voices are higher pitched. The song is faster, as young creatures move much more quickly than adult or mature creatures.)

Teaching tips

- When you sing the song in different ways, talk about how musical elements are affected, eg
  – change in speed (tempo);
  – change in quality of the voice (timbre);
  – change in pitch.

Teaching tips

It might be helpful to write a list of the following musical elements on the board to help the children when considering these questions and inventing their gnu walks:

- pitch - higher or lower sounds
- rhythm - patterns of long and short sounds played within a steady beat
- timbre - the characteristic quality of the sound produced
- tempo - the speed of the music
- duration - the length of a sound or silence

2 Discuss how the music describes the way the gnu moves

p56 77

- Listen again to *A gnu (track 77)* and ask the children to suggest the size of the animal.
  (The music is thin and light which might imply that the animal is not overweight, but the melody might indicate a fairly large animal because it starts with low notes and moves to quite high notes.)
- Ask how the music suggests the way the gnu moves.
  (There is a lively rhythm which indicates an agile animal. The melody covers a wide range, but there are no big leaps to suggest the animal jumps.)
- Show the children the picture of a gnu on the ***Picture gallery*** photocopiable and ask whether it looks how they imagined.

3 Invent a gnu walk to fit with the song, *A gnu*

77

- In pairs, the children work out suitable and imaginative movements to represent a gnu walking. Some pairs might like to invent a movement that each of them can perform separately, others might like to team up and use the four legs they have between them. They create a movement pattern which is then repeated. Encourage the children to think about the speed of the gnu's walk and the length of its stride.
  (As they work out their gnu walk, play the CD track regularly to ensure the walk fits with the music, and also to listen for rhythmic patterns that may be included in the walk.)
- Each pair performs their walk to the class whilst the class sing the song.

Picture gallery

Gnu

Bellipong

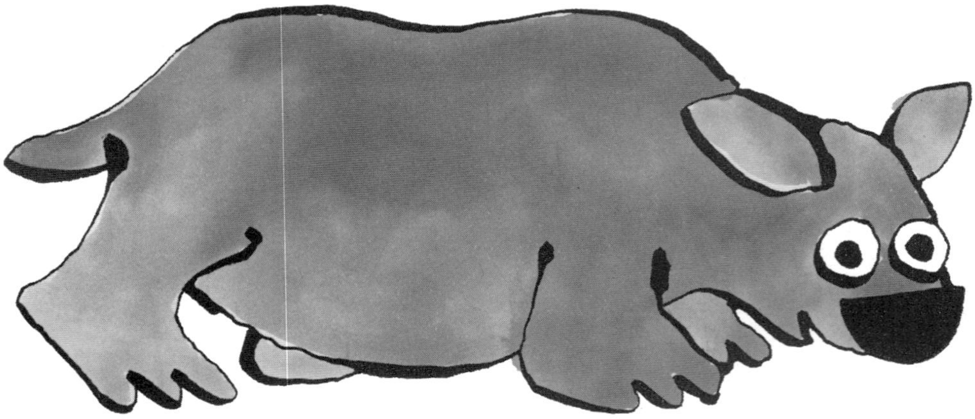

Zippi

BELLIPONG AND ZIPPI

1 Move in character to the music of *The bellipong* and *The zippi*

p56 76 80

- Listen again to *The bellipong (track 76).*
- Show the children the picture of the bellipong on the ***Picture gallery*** photocopiable. Explain that this is an artist's impression of what the bellipong looks like.
- Listen to the song again, and as you listen, all mime walking as a bellipong in time with the music.
- Listen to ***The zippi*** *(track 80)*. Ask the children if they can hear any similarities between this song and ***The bellipong.***
  *(These two songs have exactly the same melody and accompaniment but they are played twice as fast in **The zippi**.)*
- Show the children the picture of the zippi on the ***Picture gallery*** photocopiable. Explain that this is an artist's impression of what the zippi looks like. Listen again to ***The zippi***, and as you listen, all mime walking as a zippi in time with the music.

Teaching tip

- Watch to see whether individuals adapt their movements to reflect the common musical idea, or whether they invent a completely new movement.

2 Learn to sing *The bellipong* and *The zippi*, then combine them

76 80-81

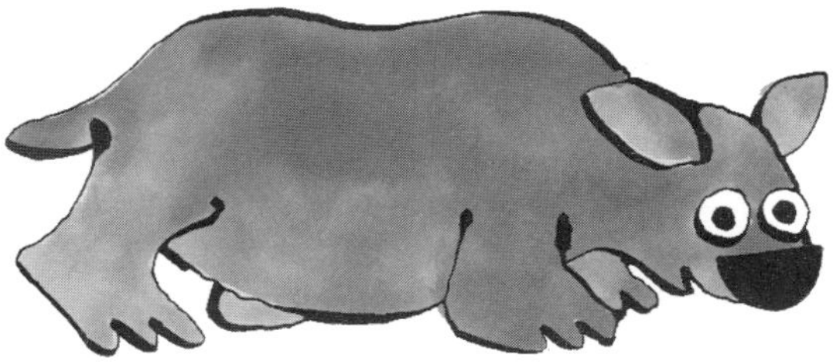

- Listen to a performance of ***The bellipong*** and ***The zippi*** sung as a duet *(track 81).*
  *(Point out that **The zippi** is sung twice in the time that **The bellipong** is sung once, because the notes of **The zippi** are played twice as fast.)*
- Divide the class in half to listen to the duet again. One half marches on the spot in time with the steady beat of ***The bellipong***, while the other half marches in time to the beat of ***The zippi***. One half should be marching twice as fast as the other.
- Teach the two songs to the children using tracks 76 and 80.

The bellipong

Fat and round, the bellipong is slow,
His tummy wobbles low, only just off the ground.

The zippi

Thin and long, the zippi whizzes past,
She's going twice as fast as the old bellipong.

- Divide the class in half to sing the two songs as a duet with track 81. One half sings ***The bellipong***, the other half sings ***The zippi***, then swap over.

Background information

- A duet is a song or piece of music for two parts of equal importance.
- A short musical idea is called a motif. It can be as short as two notes. It is like a physical gesture in dance.
- A pentatonic scale has only five different notes - the Greek word 'pent' means five.

3 Invent musical motifs for *The bellipong* and *The zippi*

81

- Ask the children to suggest some characteristic movements for each animal *(eg the bellipong might make a long, slow yawn and the zippi might scratch quickly and repeatedly).*
- Invite individuals to invent a musical motif to represent the movements suggested using the notes of the C pentatonic *(C D E G A). (They might play each note of the C pentatonic scale in turn, up then down, to represent a yawn, or one note repeated very quickly to represent scratching ...)*
- Invite volunteers to choose their favourite motif to play while the rest of the class sing ***The bellipong*** and ***The zippi*** duet with the backing track.

ANIMAL CONSEQUENCES

1 Play the game *Animal consequences* to invent new animals

- Divide the class into groups of four. Each group has an A4 sheet of plain paper folded into three to play the game:
  - the first person opens the paper and in the top section secretly draws an animal head *(the animal is totally imaginary so the head should be as creative as possible).* They then fold the top section backwards to hide the work and pass the paper to the second person;
  - the second person draws a body then folds the middle section backwards and passes it to the third person;
  - the third person draws legs and then passes the paper to the fourth person;
  - the fourth person opens the paper and shares the new animal with the group.
- Once each group has completed their new animal they suggest names for the new species they have created. The fourth member of the group makes the final choice.

2 Create a factfile about each animal's appearance, movements, personality and habits

p59

- Groups of six to eight choose any of the made-up animals from activity 1. They discuss their animal and create a factfile about it using the ***Invented animals*** photocopiable. Encourage the children to be imaginative and think about as many different features as possible, eg
  - Physical appearance
    how large or small the animal is;
    what the texture of it's coat or skin is like, eg scratchy, smooth, scaly, soft, dry, sticky ...
  - Movements
    whether the animal generally moves quickly or slowly, with an even or jumpy rhythm, noisily or quietly, with long or short strides, with light, gentle movements or heavy or aggressive movements;
    whether it makes any particular repeated movements, eg bobbing its head up and down as it walks ...
  - Personality
    what the main characteristics of its personality are ...
  - Habits
    what interesting habits the animal has ...
- Each group then starts making a note on the adjacent side of the photocopiable, of musical ideas to represent these features *(eg a large animal - low pitched sounds; moves around by jumping - low note to high note on tuned percussion; moves quickly - choose a fast tempo; is always scratching - play cabassa ...).*

3 Invent movements to reflect the animal's attributes

- Each group devises whole body movements to characterise their animal, using their factfiles for reference. Each member of the group learns to perform the animal movements.
- Each group makes a note of their animal movements - if possible video the movements.

Teaching tip

- The children will need to work in a large space to invent their animal movements.

Invented animals

FACTFILE

Our animal is the ______________________

Physical appearance:	Musical ideas:
Movements:	Musical ideas:
Personality:	Musical ideas:
Habits:	Musical ideas:

MAY I PRESENT?

1 Invent *Animal presentations* which combine music, movement and narration

p59

- Explain that each animal invented by the class is a new species. Each group will create an ***Animal presentation*** to present as full a description of their invented animal as possible using music, movement and narration.
- The narration they write should aim to present their animal as fully as possible, following the information created in their factfile last lesson, as well as being as interesting or entertaining as possible. Encourage the children to imagine the unusual, eg

  I would like to present the Chippo to you.
  Chippo loves eating cauliflowers.
  A chippo's day involves bouncing around looking for cauliflowers.
  When it sees a cauliflower, its eyes pop out of its head.
  Watch it perform its pre-eating dance ...
- Once each group has completed a narration, they choose a member of the group to be the narrator and another to mime being the animal. Everyone else will reflect the mime and narration in music.
- Each group revises their animal movements from last lesson, and considers more musical ideas for their presentations, such as:
  - which instruments to use;
  - how many different instruments are needed for each effect;
  - how they play each instrument to best convey the size and personality of the animal;
  - whether there are any keyboard or vocal sound effects that would be appropriate ...

2 Rehearse the *Animal presentations*

- Each group rehearses their ***Animal presentation.*** They should make sure that:
  - the music reflects the movement and narration;
  - the music, movement and narration is perfectly coordinated;
  - their presentation is as imaginative, informative and entertaining as possible.

3 Perform the *Animal presentations*

p59

- Each group performs their ***Animal presentation*** to the class.
- The class compare the performances with the factfiles about each animal to see how effectively the groups presented their animals. Consider in particular:
  - whether the movement implied the size of animal specified;
  - whether the movements took on the personality of the animal;
  - whether the music implied the size and personality specified;
  - whether the narration was interesting to listen to and well delivered.

Teaching tips

- Have copies of each group's factfile for the class to refer to when they watch the performances.
- Encourage the children watching to assess how creative each group has been in their *Animal presentation.*

ANIMAL COMPETITION

1 Prepare for a *Made-up animals competition*

p59

- Explain that each group is entering their made-up animal into a competition to demonstrate that it is the most fantastic animal in existence. Discuss the competition procedure. Explain that:
  - two animals at a time will come face to face and attempt to outdo each other;
  - the objective is for each group to exaggerate how fantastic their new species is through movement, narration and music;
  - the narrator will make boastful claims about their animal, which will be reflected by the person miming and by the music.
- Each group chooses one person to mime and another to interpret the mime with narration. The rest of the group reflect the mime and narration with music.
- Prepare an invitation to the headteacher or other member of the school to judge the competition.
- Each group might prepare a portfolio of their animal which includes the picture and factfile for the judge to view.

Teaching tips

- Decide as a class how many rounds the competition will have.
- If possible, arrange for the competition to take place in a large space.
- Encourage each group to keep their ideas secret from other groups during the preparation time.

2 Prepare for the *Made-up animals competition*

- Explain that each group will be put on the spot to invent ideas as they go along, but they should consider in advance:
  - their animal's strengths;
  - how they can exaggerate aspects of the animal's personality;
  - how they will work as a team to perform the movement, narration and music.

  Explain that groups will be awarded bonus marks by the judge for keeping true to their animal's personality as described by their factfiles.
- Each group works on ideas for the competition.

Teaching tips

- Make the judge aware that each group has previously given their animal a personality and set of movements. The judge should notice the groups that manage to remain in character despite being thrown off guard by the other contestant.
- Ask the judge to consider all aspects of the performance when making the decision - in particular how well the music reflects the movement and narration.

3 Perform movement, narration and music in the *Made-up animals competition*

- The judge watches pairs of groups at a time compete against each other in the *Made-up animals competition.*
- Ask the judge to give positive feedback about each group and then indicate their reasons for the overall winner.
  (If possible, video the competition so that the children can watch it afterwards and appraise their own efforts.)

Index

Index of song titles and first lines

Index of listening tracks

Videoclips

There are 17 videoclips for teachers (see introduction notes p6).

Audio CD track list

Track	Contents
	Play it again
1	Play in the gap (page 8)
2	Play in the gap example (8)
3	***Kartal*** extract (8)
4	Chiacona melodic ostinato (8)
5	Chiacona melodic ostinato sung (8)
6	***Chiacona*** extract (8)
7	***Suo-gân*** in English and in Welsh (9)
8	***Suo-gân*** first half (9)
9	***Suo-gân*** second half (9)
10	'Now with me' ostinato (9)
11	'Sleep now' ostinato (9)
12	***Suo-gân*** backing track (9)
13	***Jelly on a plate*** verse 1 (11)
14	***Jelly on a plate*** - four verses (11)
15	***Unsquare dance*** extract (13)
16	Unsquare dance ostinato 1 (13)
17	Unsquare dance – two ostinatos (13)
18	Seven square backing track (13)
19	***I'm a hip hoppy kid*** (15)
20	***I'm a hip hoppy kid*** + counted beats (15)
21	***I'm a hip hoppy kid*** backing track (15, 17)
22	***I'm a hip hoppy kid*** rhythm patterns (15)
	The class orchestra
23	***Freedom*** (18)
24	***Ki yo wah ji neh*** (18, 19)
25	***Sambalele*** (18)
26	***Did the rum do?*** (18)
27	***Ki yo wah ji neh*** phrases (19)
28	***Ki yo wah ji neh*** phrases 2 and 4 (19)
29	***Christmas calypso*** (21, 22, 23)
30	***Christmas calypso*** chorus phrases (21)
31	***Christmas calypso*** verse phrases (21)
32	***Christmas calypso*** verse 1 + chorus (22)
33	***Christmas calypso*** verse 1, phrase 1 (23)
34	***Christmas calypso*** verse 1, phrase 2 (23)
35	***Christmas calypso*** verse 1 phrases (23)
36	***Christmas calypso*** backing track (25)
	Dragon scales
37	***Jibber jabber*** - instrumental version (26, 34)
38	***Steps*** (26)
39	***Steps*** – sung version (26)
40	***Gavotte*** (26)
41	***Simple melody*** (27)
42	***Simple melody*** altered (27)
43	***Playing intervals*** backing track (27)
44	***Skye boat song*** (29)
45	***Skye boat song*** verse (29)
46	***You can do it*** (30)
47	***Do-re-mi*** - first melody (30)
48	Tonic Sol-fa scale (30)
49	***Do-re-mi*** - second melody (30)
50	***Do-re-mi*** (33)
51	***Do-re-mi*** - melodic ostinato (33)
52	***Do-re-mi*** - backing track (33)
53	***Jibber jabber*** (34)
54	***Jibber jabber*** - second voice part (34)
55	***Jibber jabber*** - xylophone melody (34)
	Painting with sound
56	***Euphoria*** extract (36)
57	***Spooky Spinney*** (36)
58	***Day off*** (37)
59	***Day off*** accompaniment (37)
60	Jogging music example (37)
61	***Seashore*** (42)
	Salt pepper vinegar mustard
62	***Crowded city*** (44)
63	Sound signals (44)
64	***Baris gede 'bandrangan'*** extract (46)
65	Five rhythm patterns (46, 47)
66	More rhythm patterns (46, 47)
67	Rhythm pattern backing track (46, 47)
68	***Inspector Morse*** opening (47)
69	***Inspector Morse*** extract (47)
70	Morse code alphabet (47)
71	'Signal' in Morse code (47)
72	***The signal song*** (49, 51, 53)
73	***The signal song*** - melody (49, 51)
74	***The signal song*** - sample lyrics (51, 53)
	Animal magic
75	***Dance of the firebird*** (54)
76	***The bellipong*** (54, 57)
77	***A gnu*** (54, 55)
78	***A gnu*** - old gnu singing (55)
79	***A gnu*** - young gnu singing (55)
80	***The Zippi*** (57)
81	***The Bellipong and the Zippi duet*** (57)

Acknowledgements

The author and publishers would like to thank all the teachers and consultants who assisted in the preparation of this series: Meriel Ascott, Francesca Bedford, Chris Bryant, Yolanda Cattle, Stephen Chadwick, Veronica Clark, Tania Demidova, Veronica Hanke, Jocelyn Lucas, Helen MacGregor, Carla Moss, Danny Monte, Lio Moscardini, Sue Nicholls, Vanessa Olney, Mrs S. Pennington, Pauline Quinton, Sheena Roberts, Ana Sanderson, Jane Sebba, Heather Scott, Michelle Simpson, Debbie Townsend and Joy Woodall. The author and publishers would like to thank Kevin Graal, Mary Medlicott, Missak Takoushian and Vivien Ellis for performing for the recording of this CD. Thanks are also due to all those who performed for previous recordings for A & C Black publications which have been reused in Music Express Year 4.

Special thanks are due to Helen MacGregor and the Year 1 and 3 children of Brunswick Park Primary School for demonstrating and performing for the filming for the CD-ROM videoclips.

The following copyright holders have kindly granted their permission for the inclusion of their copyright material in the book and on the CD:

A gnu. Words by Michael Flanders. Music by Donald Swann © 1974 The Estate of Michael Flanders and Donald Swann. Reproduced by permission of International Music Publications Ltd. All Rights Reserved.

Baris gede 'bandrangan'. King Record Co Ltd, Japan for Gamelan Gong Kebyar of "Eka Cita" (Baris gede 'bandrangan') Abian Kapas Kaja from © CD KICC 5154. Licensed by King Record Co Ltd, Japan.

Chiacona extract from HMSC Grand Tour performed by His Majesty's Sagbutts and Cornetts. Cat no 66847. Courtesy of Hyperion Records Ltd, London.

Crowded city © Barry Gibson 2001, sQuarish Productions. Copyright control.

Day off © copyright 1997 Malcolm Abbs.

Did the rum do? Kevin Graal and Folktracks & Soundpost Publications/Seamus Ennis.

Do-re-mi from 'The Sound of Music'. Lyrics by Oscar Hammerstein II. Music by Richard Rodgers. Copyright © 1959 by Richard Rodgers and Oscar Hammerstein II. Copyright Renewed. WILLIAMSON MUSIC owner of publication and allied rights throughout the world. International Copyright Secured. All Rights Reserved.

Euphoria track 5 CD-KS 1004 Percussion Around the World. © Saydisc Records. Used with permission.

I'm a hip hoppy kid by Kirtiss Horswell from 'Verse Universe'. Reproduced by kind permission of Fleetway Editions.

Inspector Morse. License courtesy of Virgin Records Ltd for theme from Inspector Morse by Barrington Pheloung from the original soundtrack CD VTCDX2 © 1991 Central Television Ltd, and by kind permission of Rainbow Music Publishing Ltd/EMI Music Publishing.

Jibber jabber. Music by Peter Gosling © Peter Gosling 1991. PFD on behalf of Michael Rosen for the adapted words from traditional © Michael Rosen.

Kartal Harmonia Mundi UK Ltd for 'Claquette-Tap dances' (*Kartal*) from Rajasthan from Musical Instruments of the World CD LX 274675 (Le Chant due Monde) ℗1990 © 1990.

Ki yo wah ji neh byJoseph Bruchac II.

Sing it on the hillside (Christmas calypso). Words by Gerry Wakelin, music by Colin Evans. Words © 1999 Gerry Wakelin, music © 1999 Colin Evans. This arrangement by Jane Sebba © 1999 A & C Black.

The firebird: Dance of the firebird performed by Bernard Haitnik. Courtesy of Phillips Music Group. Licensed by kind permission from the Film & TV Licensing division, part of the Universal Music Group.

The signal song by Maureen Hanke. © Maureen Hanke 2002, A & C Black Publishers Ltd.

Unsquare dance by Dave Brubeck. Performed by the Dave Brubeck Quartet (Dave Brubeck, Paul Desmond, Joe Morello and Eugene Wright); copyright © 1962 Derry Music Company, USA; International Copyright Secured; used with permission.

You can do it. Words and music by Jane Sebba © 1999 by Faber Music Ltd. Reproduced by permission of the publishers.

Seashore is by Nadya Kassam.

All other recordings are © A & C Black: ***Sambalele,*** collected by Claudia da Silva, ***Simple melody*** by Maureen Hanke, ***Spooky Spinney*** and ***Steps*** by David Moses, and ***The bellipong*** and ***The zippi*** by Jane Sebba.

Freedom, Gavotte, Jelly on a plate, Skye boat song, and ***Suo-gân*** are all traditional songs, arranged and recorded by A & C Black.

The game ***Tambourine talk*** is by Helen MacGregor.